Intimate Betrayal:

Hope and Healing for
Couples Recovering from
Infidelity & Sexual Addiction

Dr. Michael Don Howard

ISBN: 1463799233
ISBN-13: 9781463799236
Library of Congress Control Number: 2011914342

Introduction

When couples consider the most difficult or potentially devastating situation that they could conceivably go through in their marriage; many, if not most, respond that infidelity tops the list. This book is designed to help couples better understand both the theoretical and practical aspects of infidelity and subsequent recovery from it. We will examine a wide variety of theoretical concepts such as the definition of infidelity and why having a definition in the first place is important, the different ways that infidelity or cheating can occur, and the reasons why people cheat. As you can imagine, these topics are incredibly complex. Adding to this complexity, we will also discuss the issue of compulsive sexuality and sexual addiction and how it relates to infidelity as a whole.

With the background information firmly in place, we will then move to a more practical discussion of steps you can personally take as a couple to recover from infidelity and sexual addiction. This information will be presented within the context of a six-phase recovery model of infidelity. These chapters will discuss important steps to consider within each phase, but will also reinforce concepts and equip you with useful tools that will assist you in making your recovery more effective and successful. Through the use of stories and real-life situations, I have attempted to make this a book that couples can relate to and that will provide you with the knowledge, principles, and tools necessary to make recovery a reality.

The final section and chapter of the book is a personal reflection or letter from me regarding the potential pitfalls and challenges facing you as you embrace a journey of healing in search of lasting hope. It is my prayer that this book, while giving you information and tools to apply in your relationship, will more importantly, give you hope. Recovery from infidelity is probably the most difficult challenge you and your spouse will ever have to face, but it can be done. You and your relationship can heal. You can have a more fulfilling and loving marriage as a result. May you find success, happiness, love, and hope as you embrace the journey of healing from infidelity.

Dedication

As a marriage and family therapist, addiction counselor, and Navy Chaplain, I am passionate about the topic of infidelity and sexual addiction. As a father and as a husband, I am perhaps zealous about it. Infidelity has become a major destructive force in the lives of thousands, if not millions of families across this great nation. I desire nothing more than for couples to experience all the joy and happiness that a great marriage can offer. It is my sincere hope and prayer that this book might play even a small part in making this possible for you.

There are many that have inspired and encouraged me throughout the writing of this book. I am grateful to all of you – those mentioned and those that aren't. I want to thank Lonna, my beautiful wife of 25+ years, for her support not only on this project, but throughout our marriage. Lonna, you are a dream come true and I am blessed to have you as my companion in life.

I also want to thank each of our beautiful and incredible children – Ila, Dawn, Kimberly, and Jonathan. You have each sacrificed a lot as you have stood by me throughout my Naval career, graduate school, and a career as a therapist. I love you all from the very bottom of my heart. You are each so very special and I love being your Dad. Watching you meet the challenges of life head-on is an awesome thing to witness and to be a part of.

I want to thank my brother Tim, whose sound and thoughtful advice has kept me grounded in reality.

I also want to thank the many couples and individuals whose stories provide the necessary back drop for this book - you inspire and motivate me. Thank-you for sharing your experiences and honoring me with the opportunity to be a part of your lives and relationships.

Finally, I want to thank God. I am so grateful for His grace, mercy and Love. I am especially grateful for my Savior, Jesus Christ and the unconditional love I experience each and every day from Him. He is the one who ultimately strengthens me and it is to Him I give the glory. He is truly an awesome God!

Table of Contents

PART I – INFIDELITY – MYTHS AND REALITIES

PART II – PHASES OF INFIDELITY RECOVERY

PART III – FINDING HOPE

Part 1

INFIDELITY – MYTHS & REALITIES

CHAPTER ONE

What Is Infidelity?

Infidelity Defined

One of the most important conversations a young couple can have is about infidelity and how they are going to define it – both individually and as a couple. Many of the couples I have counseled have never thought about having such a conversation, yet alone actually doing so. You may be asking yourself, "why is this conversation important?" The question of what infidelity is sounds easy enough on the surface to answer, but as you start to "peel the onion," we find that isn't really the case. The problem is that individuals differ in their answers to this question and couples oftentimes assume that their partner has the same perceptions, thoughts, or opinions as they do on the subject. Standby for a serious dose of reality.

When I have asked couples this question, I sometimes get men who respond by saying "infidelity involves penetration." Seeking clarification and perhaps a little provocation as well, I asked, "So in order for something to be considered cheating, penetration must be involved." To this, the now confused young man responds somewhat reluctantly, "sure, absolutely – I think so." Turning to the now furious wife, I ask her for a definition of infidelity, which she responds to by saying, "anything that breaks the bond of trust between the couple or that violates the vows they took on their wedding day." As you can see from this short conversation, "Houston, we have a problem."

In abstract terms, infidelity is difficult to define and even more difficult to apply in real world situations. Couples need a practical, easy-to-understand way of determining when something could be considered cheating or not. You are probably thinking to yourself, "This should be obvious." Perhaps that is true, but people cheat every day and many of these individuals do so without realizing that the behavior could be considered wrong or inappropriate. In the above example, the wife or female partner has highlighted a common perception among women and infidelity – namely, that infidelity involves a breaking of trust or commitment. In the case of men, infidelity is seen as involving physical touch. In other words, to cheat, I must actually physically do something to another person. Kissing, fondling, oral sex, or intercourse may be examples of these more physical types of behavior. One or all of these may fit the definition – depending on the specific individual involved. There have been many people, from celebrities to high school and even middle school students who have stated that oral sex is not sex because it does not involve intercourse (which they narrowly define sex to be). The key point is that infidelity or cheating is defined by the individual, or ideally, the couple.

One of the best definitions I have heard regarding infidelity or cheating is "doing something that you would not do with your spouse or partner present." This definition accounts for a wide variety of behaviors and also speaks to the deceit and betrayal that permeates the whole concept of infidelity. From this, it is important for couples to define specific behaviors that they feel would be considered cheating. The problem, as alluded to previously, is that most couples don't discuss these things until it is too late.

Look at the list below (not necessarily all-inclusive) and circle the number(s) next to the behaviors that you would consider to be cheating. Once this is complete, you and your spouse / partner should sit down together and compare lists. Be sure to discuss your thoughts and feelings surrounding each item and *why* you feel it would be cheating.

Is it Cheating?

1. Sending an e-mail to an old girlfriend / boyfriend

2. Receiving an e-mail from an old girlfriend / boyfriend

3. Texting with an old girlfriend / boyfriend

4. Talking to an old girlfriend / boyfriend on the phone

5. Talking to an individual of the opposite sex on the phone

6. Having lunch with an old girlfriend / boyfriend

7. Having lunch with a co-worker of the opposite sex

8. Staying late to work on a project with a co-worker of the opposite sex

9. Going on a business trip with a co-worker of the opposite sex

10. E-mailing or chatting with individuals that you met online who happen to be of the opposite sex

11. Looking at dating sites to simply see if you recognize anyone or what type of people just happen to be there

12. Playing online games (non-sexual) with individuals of the opposite sex

13. Holding hands with an old girlfriend / boyfriend

14. Hugging or kissing an old boyfriend / girlfriend

15. Holding hands with an individual of the opposite sex

16. Kissing an individual of the opposite sex

17. Touching or being touched in a flirtatious manner by an individual of the opposite sex

18. Dancing with a person of the opposite sex

19. Buying or receiving a drink for or from someone of the opposite sex

20. Buying or receiving a gift for or from a person of the opposite sex

21. Looking at pornography alone (no masturbation involved)

22. Looking at pornography with your spouse or partner (no masturbation involved)

23. Looking at pornography with a group of friends (no masturbation involved)

24. Looking at pornography while masturbating (alone)

25. Looking at pornography while masturbating (with spouse or partner)

26. Looking at pornography while masturbating (in a group)

27. Sending or receiving sexual pictures

28. Engaging in sexual chat or e-mail with someone online

29. Giving or receiving oral sex with someone of the opposite sex

30. Giving or receiving oral sex with someone of the same sex

31. Having intercourse with someone of the opposite sex

32. Having intercourse with someone of the same sex

33. Having oral sex with a third person with your spouse or partner present

34. Having intercourse with a third person with your spouse or partner present

35. Having oral sex with another couple with your spouse or partner present

36. Having intercourse with another couple with your spouse or partner present

37. Attending a group sex party with your spouse or partner

38. Using toys (vibrators, dildos, dolls) when spouse or partner not present

39. Using toys (vibrators, dildos, dolls) when spouse or partner is present

40. Going to a strip club without spouse or partner

41. Going to strip club with spouse or partner

42. Giving or receiving oral sex when spouse or partner is unavailable (business trip, vacation, military deployment)

43. Having intercourse when spouse or partner is unavailable (business trip, vacation, military deployment)

44. Receiving a lap dance at a strip club

45. Attending a bachelor / bachelorette party with exotic dancers / strippers are present

46. Paying for sex with a prostitute or escort

Couples need to recognize the need to have this conversation. It is extremely likely that you and your partner have different ideas regarding what specific behaviors constitute cheating. At least by having the conversation, you can't say "I didn't know you felt that way."

I was counseling a young Marine couple years ago because the wife felt that her husband had a problem with pornography. I recall during the first or second session asking her whether she considered it to be cheating. Her response was as I expected it to be, "yes! Of course it is." I thought the husband was going to come unglued. He thought she was over-reacting and exaggerating the situation and her feelings in order to receive sympathy points.

He felt that she was completely out of touch with contemporary society and what men do. To him, pornography was acceptable and was just something that men do. It is an activity like playing cards or videogames – to pass the time. He simply could not understand what she was feeling and did not see the incredible hurt and pain that it caused her.

Fast forward about a month later and you would have thought I was sitting with a completely different couple. He started by telling me that he finally "got it." When I asked him to clarify, he said it was like a light switch came on and he was beginning to see why his wife was so hurt by the pornography. She smiled and told me that they had gone through their entire house together - room by room, removing and destroying any material that was inappropriate or even questionable. The best part was that it was his idea. She talked about how good that felt and how she finally felt that he was starting to understand the impact this has had on her and on their marriage. They also told me that he went to work early one day and removed every bit of porn from the office – regardless of who it actually belonged to. He remarked that several of his colleagues were not happy.

So what can we learn from this story? First, couples may have different ideas with regards to what constitutes infidelity or cheating. This is highlighted by the fact that this particular man saw nothing wrong with looking at and collecting pornography. These male / female gender differences are not uncommon. Second, it took a while before the husband realized that his behavior was a problem. He initially felt as though it was simply his wife that had the problem (in not accepting his culturally acceptable behavior) and that if she would get over it, all would be well. Therefore, patience is required in the early phases of treatment or counseling because it may take a while for some level of accountability to set in. Finally, for the person who is acting out (viewing pornography in this case) to truly want to change, he or she needs to see and "feel" how this behavior is impacting his or her partner. If they get to the point where they see it, but just don't care then there are other problems or issues. The husband in this case finally saw the deep pain that he had caused his wife and was disgusted by his actions and the idea that he could actually hurt her like this.

It is important to understand that infidelity does not have to involve sexual behavior. Sex may be part of it, but it doesn't have to be. Just look at the list of behaviors on the cheating list discussed earlier in this chapter. Many of those behaviors are not sexual in nature. Sex is oftentimes the outcome that gets the attention because it is high-energy, emotional, and political. It creates interesting conversation. Sex is also something that many feel is reserved exclusively for them and it is therefore considered sacred. It is included in our wedding vows so it must be important. It may surprise you to think that simply talking, texting, or having lunch with a person of the opposite gender could be considered cheating. Let's take a look at Jim and Sarah.

Jim was a young Marine who had come to see me because of a pornography addiction. He had approximately five thousand images saved on his computer. He would routinely look at these images or watch pornographic videos online that he had received from friends. Although Jim would engage in this behavior almost every night for hours at a time, he did not feel that he had a problem. Sarah had serious issues with his behavior, but she responded in an enabling, co-dependent manner by serving him dinner in the living room at the computer; allowing him to access pornography right there in the living room, on the computer in front of her; and even allowing him to sleep in the living room under the computer table on occasion. Additional information on co-dependency and enabling behavior will be presented in chapter four.

Although it took many months, Jim eventually stopped looking at pornography and even deleted every image and video off of his computer. We were having a counseling session one day about a month or two later during which Sarah informed me that Jim had been cheating on her. Jim looked up at the ceiling, folded his arms, rolled his eyes, and said "here we go again." I asked Sarah to say more about this. She proceeded to tell me that earlier in the week, she had walked into the living room where Jim was on the computer playing an online game and having a conversation with a woman in Europe. He had never met this woman and by all accounts, probably never would. Sarah looked at the conversation on the screen and accused Jim of cheating. He looked at her as though she was crazy and asked how it could be cheating when there was nothing sexual at all in the conversation. Sarah then said that he was having a conversation with another woman that he had never had with her, his own wife. The conversation was about his job and his feelings about being a Marine. This couple helped me to see how such an innocuous or seemingly innocent behavior could be considered to be cheating and how much pain, hurt, and devastation can result from it. We can't afford to take these behaviors for granted.

Another factor to consider when talking about infidelity is the aspect of secrecy or deceit. I have had many spouses tell me that almost any behavior, if kept secret, could potentially be problematic. For example, my wife might be okay with me having lunch with a female co-worker if I tell her about it either ahead of time or at the first opportunity afterwards. She would likely not be okay with it if she hears about the luncheon from a friend who happened to see us together. People do not like being lied to and deceit and secrecy are both forms of lying.

Years ago, when I graduated from Naval Chaplain School, a good friend of ours flew out to our home in Maine to travel with us to Illinois where we were moving. This friend was a woman who grew up with my wife and was now divorced. I was going to pick her up at the airport in Rhode Island upon leaving Chaplain School and we would then drive to our home in Maine. The flight wasn't going to land until about midnight and then it would be a five or six hour drive home. Knowing this, I asked my wife ahead of time if she minded if this friend and I stopped at a hotel for the night. She had no problem with it. I also asked her if she minded if I only got one room in order to save money. Again, she had no problem with it. I then asked her to call her friend and see if she had any objections. She was fine with it as well. To make a long story short, I picked our friend up at the airport as scheduled, we stayed the night in a hotel, and we drove to Maine the next day.

Had I not asked my wife ahead of time and simply stopped for the night, she may have had a huge problem. She may have even considered it to be cheating. Nothing happened and I recalled later how convenient and even tempting such a situation could be. It was not smart and I would probably not do it again – just to avoid temptation or even the perception of doing something inappropriate. Thankfully, my wife trusted both me and our friend. I know for a fact that our friend would never do anything to hurt my wife, but I remember telling my wife that she trusts me more than I trust myself. Trust is important, but we should not take it for granted and should avoid putting ourselves in tempting situations unnecessarily.

Having explored and discussed the question of what infidelity is (and isn't), let's now examine the different types of infidelity in greater detail. Before doing so however, take a few minutes and respond to the following questions:

Exercise

Questions for Consideration: Answer each question to the best of your ability, being as thorough as possible in your response.

1. How would you define infidelity? In what ways do you feel that your spouse's definition is similar and/or different from yours? What do you feel accounts for any differences between these definitions of infidelity? What would you like to say to your spouse about defining infidelity that you haven't yet?

2. Assuming that an infidelity has occurred, how has it changed your relationship? In what ways has it altered your view of the meaning of marriage? How has it impacted your perception of yourself and your spouse?

3. Taking into consideration those things that were discussed in this chapter, what have you found most helpful and why? How might having a practical definition of infidelity help you in your relationship today? What could you do today that would positively impact your marriage with regards to the topic of infidelity?

CHAPTER TWO

Types Of Infidelity

As you will recall from our discussion of the question "what is infidelity?" in the previous chapter, infidelity can take many different forms and much of what is or is not considered infidelity is the subjective opinion of the person or people involved. In this chapter, we are going to begin organizing these different forms of infidelity into groups that will enable us to better understand the causes and potential treatment implications for the various behaviors involved.

At the broadest level, we can divide infidelity into two categories: (1) physical and (2) cyber or technological related behaviors. I am reluctant to use the word affair because affair, to me, implies a relationship, whether one-time or on-going. Infidelity can also be broken up into the medium used. For example, there is physical infidelity which involves actually touching or being with another person; there is cyber-infidelity which can involve e-mail, chatting, use of dating sites, webcams, and pornography. It may or may not involve sexual acting out or sexually explicit text. There is also infidelity that can occur through the use of cell phones, which could also involve the cyber-infidelity behaviors just mentioned. Phones, for purposes of this discussion will involve actual talking and/or texting. Finally, infidelity can involve hand-written letters or notes. What is perhaps most important to realize at this point however, is that although infidelity can take many different forms, the pain involved and the potential devastation to the marriage or relationship is essentially the same.

Physical Infidelity

Physical infidelity involves any behavior in which a person in a committed relationship breaks the trust of that relationship by engaging in a sexual or even non-sexual relationship or activities with another person outside of that relationship. For ease of discussion, I will begin with what most people would simply call an affair. An affair can begin in many different ways and can take many different paths depending on the individuals involved and circumstances surrounding it. Affairs typically begin with two people who begin spending time together because of work, school, and shared interests stemming from social organizations, family and child activities, church functions, and various levels of friendship and interaction.

Example of a Traditional Affair

Let's examine one hypothetical affair as an illustration. Mark and Stefanie are co-workers who have been assigned to work on an important marketing project together. Mark is 38 years old and has been married for ten years. Stefanie is 26 years old and has been married for four years. Mark and his wife, Linda, have three children and Stefanie and her husband, Brad, have one. Mark and Stefanie have known each other for about two years, but this is the first project they have worked on together. The project requires them to spend a lot of time together both at work and after hours. As they begin spending time together working on the project, they begin to discover they have many things in common and are enjoying spending time together. As the time they spend together increases, they find themselves having lunch together, drinks after work, and the conversation starts to become more personal and intimate as well. There is more flirtatious behavior and even colleagues at work have noticed how close and comfortable Mark and Stefanie have become with one another.

In the course of their working together, Stefanie has come to really admire Mark; particularly his wisdom, work ethic, and confidence. Likewise, Mark has come to enjoy Stefanie's eagerness, enthusiasm, humor, intellect, and physical beauty. As the conversation continues to become more personal, Mark shares how dissatisfied he is in his marriage and how he wishes his wife was more like Stefanie. Stefanie loves the way Mark talks to her and wishes her husband would open up and share his feelings like Mark does. She feels that Brad does not notice her and is preoccupied with his work, hobbies, and guy friends. Mark and Stefanie continue to grow closer, enjoying their time together and flirting with one another every chance they get. After about 2-3 months, the project is nearing completion and they make plans for a business trip to a large city for three days to make presentations to potential clients.

The trip begins innocently enough and the presentations go remarkably well with the company landing a major account. To celebrate, Mark and Stefanie go out to dinner and then spend several hours dancing, drinking, and talking before returning to the hotel. On their way up to their rooms in the elevator, Mark hugs Stefanie and tells her how happy and lucky he is to have her as a friend and as a co-worker. The hug turns into a kiss and instead of returning to their own rooms, they go together to his room and enjoy a night of passionate love-making. The sexual relationship continues throughout the rest of the trip. Although they do feel guilty after returning home, the affair continues for the next six months until Linda, Mark's wife, discovers some provocative text messages and e-mails between Mark and Stefanie. She confronts Mark and the affair is now in the open.

Characteristics of an Affair

This story highlights several dynamics that typically occur when a physical affair has occurred. First, for an affair to occur there must be opportunity. Opportunity presented itself in this case as Mark and Stefanie were put in close proximity for a work project, having to spend a lot of time together – including afterhours and even traveling out of town. This does not mean that men and women can't work together, but it does mean that additional precautions may need to be taken. Affairs in the workplace are common. We see it in all sectors of society from government to the private sector. It is also worth noting that these affairs can involve same sex partners as well.

The second dynamic highlighted in the story of Mark and Stefanie is how their conversation shifted over time. It likely began very professional with superficial discussion of family and personal issues. With time however, that changed and they found themselves becoming much more personal in their conversation, as well as joking and flirting with one another. As people become more comfortable with and around one another, they will engage in more personal conversation and behavior. In many cases, this level of comfort will allow individuals to take relational risks that they may not otherwise take, assuming that the other person is receptive to a deeper or more intimate relationship.

A third dynamic and one that is somewhat related to that just previously discussed has to do with vulnerability and sharing of feelings related to self, the marriage, and other parts of one's personal and/or professional life. For example, in the case presented, Mark shared with Stefanie how dissatisfied he was in his marriage and how he wished his wife was more like Stefanie. Similarly, Stefanie let Mark know how much she admired him and that unlike her husband Brad, Mark opened up and willingly shared his feelings with her. This was something she longed for, but could not get at home.

These were two vulnerable people who began to see things in each other that they deeply desired from their spouse. It is common to see things we appreciate in people we admire, like, or are attracted to. As they got closer and the opportunity presented itself, Mark and Stefanie were thrust into a sexual affair that lasted many months. It is also worth mentioning that although this affair was a sexual one, it was grounded heavily in an emotional relationship. These two individuals were not simply looking for sex; they wanted to fulfill their deeper emotional needs and sought out a sexual relationship in an effort to make that happen. They were feeling lonely, unappreciated, unloved, taken for granted, and relationally unfulfilled in their marriages. They were also experiencing the "grass is greener on the other side of the fence phenomena" by being with one another and saw each other as the answer to their problems. Through each other, they sought to have their emotional (and physical) needs met.

Continuing with our discussion of vulnerabilities and emotional needs, Mark was probably very excited that a beautiful, young, intelligent woman would take such an interest in him. In some ways it was just the validation he was looking for – as a man and as a working professional. Stefanie was impressed with Mark's business sense, his experience, and the way he coordinated the project. She probably saw him in some ways as the kind of executive she wanted to be. She also saw a different side of him however - the caring, loving, sensitive man that would open up to her and listened to her and what she was feeling and experiencing. She wanted this from her own husband, but he either didn't know how, was unwilling, or was not aware of her needs. Regardless, she found what she needed from Mark.

Every couple that I have counseled that has had an affair has done so because of vulnerabilities and opportunities. I personally think that these vulnerabilities are at the root of the behavioral issue. If couples could identify the vulnerabilities within themselves, each other, and the relationship and communicate their needs to each other in a meaningful way then our perceived need for an affair would go away or at least be sharply diminished and it would not matter as much whether opportunities present themselves or not. We will discuss this concept more extensively in part two of the book.

One-night Stands

In addition to the traditional off-line or real-time affair discussed already, individuals can also engage in physical infidelity in the form of one-night stands. Although the specific behaviors can vary greatly, the basic premise is that the person is not looking so much for a relationship or new partner, as much as he or she is looking for companionship or in some cases, simply sex. Like other types of affairs however, one-night stands almost always involve sexual acting out (although they don't necessarily have to). Let's look at some of the more common types of one-night stands.

Prostitution

One type of one-night stand that more commonly occurs with men than women is paying for sex. This involves finding a woman (or man) to have sex with or to go on a "date" with. This can most easily be accomplished by going online to escort service sites and simply "booking a date." These sites will have basic information about the escorts, pictures, availability, and in some cases, the fees that are charged. Escorts can be affiliated with an agency or work independently. They also differ in terms of whether they offer in-call (in which the client travels to them) or out-call (in which the escort comes to the client – usually at a home or hotel). Many of these escorts will take credit cards as a form of payment in addition to cash. The sex can take many different variations and some will engage in role-play or other types of specific fetishes; such as sadomachism, cross-dressing, and bondage; depending on the preferences of the client. Clients typically pay by the hour (or half-hour), although multiple-hour and over-night dates are usually offered as well.

Many female escorts specialize in providing what is referred to as the "girlfriend experience" (GFE). It still involves a sexual encounter and is typically booked by the hour. With this type of date however, the escort attempts to create an environment similar to what might be found with a girlfriend or on a regular date. There might be more conversation, body rubs, the couple might shower or bathe together, and there will likely be more foreplay and kissing. This type of experience attracts men who are lonely and who are looking for human connection at various levels. Although considered a one-night stand, the goal of most escorts is to create a clientele consisting of repeat customers.

In addition to escorts who advertise online, there are also more traditional types of prostitution in which men and women stand on corners or walk certain parts of town looking for customers or "Johns." These prostitutes are usually referred to as "streetwalkers" or "whores" and are typically found in red-light districts or parts of town known for prostitution and drug activity. Encounters with these types of prostitutes are almost always for purely physical or sexual purposes. They last a much shorter period of time and will often take place in a car, motel room, or in an alley or park. As opposed to escorts, there is little to no real intimacy in these encounters. The price is much cheaper as well, with some prostitutes charging $20 or less as opposed to escorts who may be charging $300-500 for an hour. The physical risk is also much higher with prostitutes on the street. They are typically less concerned with safety which subsequently causes the rate of sexually-transmitted diseases to be much higher.

Strip Clubs

For some individuals, going to a strip club can be considered infidelity (even though no touching may occur). Many men get themselves in trouble with wives and girlfriends by going to strip clubs with a group of guys or as part of a bachelor party or other celebration. The biggest mistake guys typically make is not telling their significant other before the fact, or at the very least, right after. As with most things, secrets make it much worse and when a group is involved, you have to know that the word is going to get out and that she fill find out.

The psychology of the strip club experience for the wife is fairly simple. She does not want her husband going someplace where he can look at young, beautiful, naked women and then subsequently fantasize about being with that person or doing things with her as opposed to being with his wife. She will feel that he is not completely committed to her, that he would rather be with someone else, or that she is somehow not good enough. She will likely feel inferior, comparing herself to these women, wondering why she is not pretty enough or sexy enough to keep her husband's attention. This experience is made even worse if he receives a lap dance in which the fantasy is heightened as the dancer focuses her attention on only one person – the husband, while rubbing up against him. Although touching during lap dances is usually not permitted, it can and does occur. Many dancers will also provide additional sexual services after hours or in a back room for additional fees. The motivating force behind the strip club for the man is visual arousal coupled with fantasy. There are also some couples who go to strip clubs together. Although it may still be fueled by fantasy and both partners are in agreement to going, I personally don't see it as a healthy thing as it can still result in a lot of the negative factors discussed earlier. The wife may agree to go simply to be able to keep an eye on him or to observe his reaction to the dancers. In my opinion, it is like playing with fire. Anytime one spouse is focusing their attention on another man or woman instead of their own husband or wife, there will be problems.

Luncheons and Friendship Dates

It is not unusual for a man and a woman who are married or in committed relationships with other people to go out to lunch or someplace else together. That does not however, mean that it is safe, free of temptation, or even wise to do so. Anytime a man and woman are alone together, there is the potential for something to happen between them. This is compounded by personal vulnerabilities and issues that they may be facing individually or relationally at home. For these reasons, many men and women make it a conscious practice to never be alone with someone of the opposite sex. I had a friend once tell me he would not even get in an elevator if it meant being alone with another woman. When I asked him about this odd form of perceived paranoia, he said that he didn't want to put himself in a position where something inappropriate could happen and he didn't want to even be in a position where someone else could wonder or perceive that something inappropriate had happened. Perhaps this is a wise practice – definitely a cautious one.

I personally don't think it is wrong for a man and woman who are married or in committed relationships to have lunch or spend time with a co-worker or friend of the opposite sex. I do however, think that there should be absolutely no secrecy, deceit, or attempt to hide the event from anyone. The individuals also need to consider perceptions others may have and factor that into an informal risk assessment. In other words, perceptions of co-workers, neighbors, or family members may make having lunch together simply too painful or have a potentially negative impact personally and/or professionally. We must remember that perception is reality.

In addition to vulnerabilities as discussed earlier, the individuals having lunch together or attending some other type of function together should consider their level of comfort and decide individually ahead of time what precautions may need to be taken, what topics are acceptable to discuss, what actions will be taken if a boundary is crossed, what locations are acceptable to meet in, and what actions will be taken if the other person becomes flirtatious or even aggressive sexually. It would be wise to also consider having limits on drinking or avoid drinking all together. The following questions may assist you in your decision making process:

1. In what ways might you be vulnerable to the affections or advances of the other person?

2. In what ways is the other person vulnerable?

3. Where are you willing to meet? Are you willing to meet at a home, hotel, or other setting where you are completely alone?

4. What precautions are you going to take with regards to alcohol?

5. How will you respond if he or she becomes overly flirtatious or makes sexual advances?

6. What topics are fair game to be discussed or conversely, are off limits?

7. How often do you feel comfortable meeting and for how long?

8. What times of day or night are acceptable for meeting?

9. What extra precautions or concerns do you have if there is a need to travel (e.g., business trip)?

10. Who needs to know about this meeting and when?

An important consideration when discussing friendship and co-worker dates or events is the intention of the two individuals involved. In other words, does one of the two want or hope that a relationship might develop? Similarly, does one of the two want to have a sexual relationship with the other? Do they fantasize about these as possibilities? If the answer to any of these questions is yes, then there is room for concern.

Dating Sites

Another type of physical infidelity that fits in the category of one-night stands is online adult dating sites, often referred to as hook-up sites. Although it involves a technological medium, it is included here because of the physical nature of the resultant behavior. These sites (such as *Adult Friend Finder* and *Craig's List*) allow individuals to post ads or profiles that other viewers can then review and subsequently make contact via e-mail, text, or phone, if they are interested in meeting (typically for the sole purpose of having sex). These sites are oftentimes free, or in some cases, have a small monthly membership fee associated with it.

These sites are also divided by target audiences or sexual preferences. For example, they are usually separated into categories such as men looking for women, women looking for men, men looking for men, and women looking for women. There are also categories for couples looking for individuals and for couples looking for other couples. The couples looking for a third person will usually attempt to exclude any married or attached individuals, but it may come as a surprise to you – people lie on their profiles. Specialty fetish sites are yet another option.

I have had many couples or individuals come to me for counseling because one of the two individuals discovered that their spouse or partner had been on an adult dating website. This is significant, because it almost always indicates a pattern of betrayal in which the person was or is looking for a sexual and/or romantic partner. In many cases, they aren't looking for a "regular" partner, but there is always a chance of that. Individuals who have gone to dating sites looking for a sexual partner have in most instances, also probably acted out in other ways. This type of discovery destroys the relational trust and the impact on the spouse who did not act out or have the affair (the injured partner) can be significant. This behavior can and oftentimes does result in post-traumatic stress disorder (PTSD) or symptoms of traumatic stress at a minimum. Recovery for the couple is possible, but it is a challenging, demanding, and painful process.

Friends with Benefits

Friends with benefits is a somewhat contemporary term that simply reflects the notion of an uncommitted or "no strings attached" sexual relationship. These types of relationships are not uncommon in young adults and even high school or middle school age adolescents. The premise with these relationships is that we can have regular consensual sex whenever we both agree without the hassle, expense, and drama associated with a real romantic relationship. There typically are no feelings of love between the two individuals, although in most instances, they are good friends and do care about one another. They do not however, have to be extremely close friends to enter into this type of relationship.

I consider this type of relationship to be somewhat of a hybrid. On one level, all the two individuals seem to want from the relationship is sex. They may hang out from time to time, but they often get together for the stated purpose of having sex or at least engaging in sexual behavior. On a deeper level however, they are choosing to have a sexual relationship with a friend because there is safety and security, as well as a level of intimacy and comfort that is not possible when having sex with a stranger. In many ways, this type of relationship mirrors that of the girlfriend experience in the earlier discussion about escorts, but without the financial and time constraints. In many ways, the friend in this type of relationship functions as a girlfriend (or boyfriend), minus the actual dating and courting behaviors. Although it is likely that most people in this type of relationship are single, it is not always the case and many times one of the two are married or in a committed relationship.

Affair partners in these types of relationships are likely to be neighbors, childhood friends, family friends, co-workers, teachers, or other individuals in whom a relationship of this type is negotiated either directly or indirectly. To some extent, it is a relationship of convenience. A key point is that these types of affairs feel very different from other types of affairs and have a very distinct purpose – one that is in stark contrast to the traditional affair between people looking for a romantic or emotional relationship.

Individuals in a friends-with-benefits type of relationship are looking for sex, but more importantly, are looking for emotional intimacy. They simply use the sexual relationship that is framed upon a safe and secure friendship to meet these emotional needs. As stated earlier, these are people that trust and care for one another. They are extremely comfortable with each other, but have no expectations of having or even wanting to have a deeper, more romantic type of relationship.

Cyber and Technological Infidelity

The second major category of infidelity is what I refer to as cyber or even technological infidelity. The distinguishing feature of this type of infidelity is that it typically does not involve physical contact with the other person and some form of technology is utilized as the medium through which the behavior takes place. In the past, some researchers and clinicians have referred to this type of behavior as emotional infidelity. Although it is grounded heavily in emotion, other forms of infidelity (such as physical affairs) can have a significant emotional piece as well.

As technology continues to advance, the opportunity to use it in harmful and destructive ways does so as well. We have seen the significant impact of the computer on the pornography industry. Cell phones are not only used for calling people, they are used for texting, sending and receiving pictures and videos, interfacing with the internet, and locating people (through GPS features) who might be interested in "hooking up" or having sex. Then we have social media sites like *My Space, Face Book, Twitter,* and *Linked In* – all used to help people stay connected to one another through the virtual world. All of these devices and features have in one way or another, been used for acting out sexually and creating yet another path through which infidelity can occur.

A few years back, my cell phone died somewhat suddenly and I decided that I really needed to replace my phone. Despite my hesitation and deep desire to procrastinate a while longer, I finally decided to take the plunge. I walked into a local cell phone store and after the young salesman asked me if he could help me, I responded, "I need to buy a new phone." He then inquired, "What would you like your phone to be able to do?" Somewhat perplexed, I thought about it for a minute, wondering if I had missed the invention of a phone that would wash my car, mow the lawn, and give a great massage after pouring me an ice cold beer. After a few seconds of this, I looked at him and said, "Well, I would like to be able to call people. I would also love it if people could call me. What the heck, might as well live on the edge - I would also like to be able to text." He smiled and said, "I think we can handle that." Needless to say, I have had the same phone since and I can still make and receive calls, as well as text. It also has a camera. I know what you are thinking – I am truly living in the fast lane. I am still waiting however, for my phone to mow the lawn and wash the car. Thankfully, I have kids to help with that.

Texting and Sexting

Two of the most popular ways that cyber-infidelity occurs is through texting and sexting. Texting is simply where two people send each other text messages via their cell phones. Billions of text messages are sent in the United States each year – at home, work, school; while driving, walking, and even while riding bicycles and motorcycles. Approximately 80% of cell phone subscribers have texting service plans. There are also increasing numbers of studies showing that texting is addictive and that it is severely impacting people's lives – positively and negatively.

In terms of infidelity, many of the couples I counsel come in because the wife (and to a lesser extent the husband) have discovered text messages between their spouse and another person of the opposite sex. These text messages do not have to be sexual in nature to be considered infidelity and for the sake of this discussion, we will assume they aren't. Sexual texts will be discussed in a few minutes when we talk about sexting. The reason texting can and oftentimes is considered to be infidelity by many individuals is that the person is having a personal, emotional, and perhaps even evocative conversation with someone other than his or her spouse. The spouse may feel that they have been replaced or that they are not as important as this other person.

Texting is so popular that many believe it is affecting the ability of some people to establish real relationships and to subsequently have meaningful conversations in a face-to-face environment. It is causing people to isolate and to withdraw into an artificial world; a world void of actual people interacting in real-life situations. The spouse who discovers the text messages is usually deeply hurt - wishing that their husband or wife would have these types of conversations or spend this amount of time with them. This type of emotional betrayal is more likely to impact women than men, and in more profound ways; but both men and women find the hurt and betrayal to be a significant factor. Texting is a way that people can have a conversation without taking risks. They can say whatever they want and like online chatting, the individual can pretend to be just about anyone they want as well. There are no non-verbal behaviors to worry about, they can't see your face, and you can edit and review every response prior to sending. It eliminates much of the risk present in other forms of communication.

Sexting is where the cell phone is used for sexually explicit purposes. For example, two people can have a sexual conversation by texting this type of content back and forth. Couples may send provocative or nude pictures to one another, and can even masturbate while doing so. Just as couples can use chatting on the internet to "have sex" with each other, individuals are using cell phones in the same manner. Many people get in trouble legally and professionally for this type of behavior. There is a Congressman in the news as I write this that recently resigned his position and may lose his marriage and his political career for sending explicit text messages and photos of himself to various women throughout the country. There have also been cases in the courts where teenagers were prosecuted for possession and distribution of child pornography because they took nude pictures of one another and sent them to other kids in their high school. These teenagers consented to the pictures and in some cases, took the pictures of themselves and forwarded them. These types of behaviors can have incredibly significant, life-changing consequences.

Years ago, I was counseling a Marine who was facing court-martial for taking nude pictures with his cell phone of his brother's fifteen year-old girlfriend. Although consensual, this was considered to be child pornography and he went to jail for it. Even simply receiving a nude picture of an underage person is considered to be possession of child pornography and is illegal. It is important to keep in mind that these behaviors are not simply destructive personally and professionally, they are against the law.

So why do people get involved in these sexting behaviors? First, I believe that it provides a means whereby people can live or act out their fantasies. They can have a sexual conversation and exchange pictures with someone they would likely never actually be able to have a sexual or romantic relationship with or would be hesitant or unwilling to attempt one with. It also minimizes and even eliminates any health concerns associated with STDs and unwanted pregnancies. I also believe that there is a power component sometimes associated with sexting in that the person may use the behavior as a means to feel better about himself, as though he is desirable or wanted, possibly even using it as a way of "conquering" another person. This is similar to a person who has sex with a lot of women and with each one, carves another notch in the bedpost. Sexting also has a more personal component, when compared to viewing pornography online or masturbating to pornography or fantasy.

Chatting

Chatting is simply where individuals use computers to speak to each other through typed messages. It is similar in many respects to texting, but a computer is used instead of a cell phone. Webcams are also oftentimes used so that the individuals involved can see one another. Chatting can occur in organized online groups or in dedicated private chats. The group chat rooms are typically structured around a theme such as a geographical location, hobby, interest, or age. These chats are not private and anyone can read them and participate in the process - sometimes by pretending to be anyone they wish. The associated anonymity makes this is a popular place for child predators to hang out.

Online chatting can be sexual or non-sexual. Like many conversations between people of the opposite sex, they may start out non-sexual and somewhat superficial, becoming increasingly provocative and explicit over time. This can occur very quickly in some instances, and it is not uncommon for couples to engage in cyber-sexual conversation and even masturbation via webcam the first time they chat online. For the married couple, catching a spouse engaging in this type of behavior would be devastating - to the individual as well as to the marriage. Even though the person isn't actually touching the other person and might never get to the point of actually meeting, they are being sexual with one another, are viewing each other in sexual acts, and are responding to sexual fantasy involving this other person or persons. One concern for the spouse is the question of how long this type of behavior has been going on, how many other people has he or she done this with, and what the likelihood is that this has or will escalate to an offline meeting. Other questions the spouse will likely have revolve around her own self-worth and include: "what is wrong with me? Am I not pretty enough, sexy enough, or good enough in bed?"

Pornography

Approximately seventy million people visit pornographic webs sites each week. Of these, twenty percent are in the United States. Most pornography is accessed during the day, which means much of it is occurring at work or by children at home after school. In fact, studies have shown that children ages 12-16 make up the largest group of pornography viewers. In many cases, this is because they are home alone while their parents are working, or they are doing homework and mistakenly stumble across an inappropriate site. Many porn sites are intentionally spelled similar to other sites with one letter being different so that a simple misspelled word can bring people to the porn site accidentally.

I counseled a teenage girl who had been referred to be by her pastor because she was supposedly viewing pornography on a regular basis. It started one day while she was online in what would have been considered a very acceptable teen chat room. One of the kids in the room challenged her to go some external sites. These happened to be hardcore porn sites consisting of daddy-daughter rape and fisting images. She immediately exited the sites, but the images were forever planted in her mind and triggered her curiosity. About three or four days later she went back to those sites. This time she became increasingly curious and even excited or intrigued by the images. This led to a pattern of exposure where she would get up around 5:00 a.m. in order to access the family computer in the living room while her parents and siblings were asleep. She would surf porn sites for about an hour or until her family began to get up. This persisted for about a month before her mom discovered what she had been doing, spoke to the pastor, and the daughter was referred to me. The point is this was a "good" girl who grew up in a value-centered, Godly home. The computer was accessible and located in a common area of the house. Her parents supervised her regular computer use and were careful about what things they typically allowed her to be exposed to. She was led astray by another child and with one exposure was essentially hooked. I am happy to report however, that she has not looked at pornography since and is doing very well now.

Many people (mostly women) feel that looking at pornography is wrong and to some, it is even considered to be infidelity or cheating. I have had many wives describe the pain, shock, and betrayal resulting from catching their husband in the middle of the night on the computer masturbating to pornographic images of other women, couples, and on rare occasions, men. The questions are the same, "Am I not pretty enough, sexy enough, or good enough in bed?" In other words, the wife takes responsibility for the behavior by thinking that there must be something wrong with them if their husband feels the need to look at pornography and masturbate to it.

Men are more likely to become aroused by visual cues and triggers. This is why men get excited over nude photos, videos, beautiful women walking along the beach, billboards, and lingerie commercials. For men, these images are like "eye candy." It has been said that men use their eyes, while women use their hearts. There is also the popular saying that men oftentimes think with their "little head." When I ask men, "When was the first time you remember looking at pornography?" I usually get replies such as "when I was about seven or eight and I discovered my dad's stash of Playboy or Penthouse magazines." The days of adult magazines are probably all but gone since the development of computers, the internet, and online porn. The net result is that internet porn is so readily available, accessible, and affordable – a term that addiction researcher Al Cooper referred to as the triple "A" engine. Kids today are being exposed to porn when doing homework, walking in on mom or dad looking at it on the computer, or possibly even seeing a picture that mom or dad received via e-mail or on their phone. I would not be surprised to discover that a majority of kids in America today are exposed to internet pornography by the age of five or six. It is estimated that 93% of children will have viewed online pornography by the time they graduate high school.

The problem with pornography is that it objectifies men and women into sexual objects. They are perceived as objects that exist for the purpose of sexual gratification, having little other value. When I was facilitating a psychoeducation group on sexual addiction with men in treatment for alcohol and /or drug addiction, I typically asked them to think about how they view women. I would say, "Are you more likely to view women as a "walking vagina" whose primary or even sole purpose is sex and to please you; or do you view women as created in the image of God, placed here to be a partner and to make your life more rewarding and joyful." In many of the groups I led, a large number stated that they were more likely to view women as "walking vaginas." This is a sad commentary on how we view women and how far we have come in our basic beliefs about men, women, and sex.

I have a lot of couples who watch porn together. My opinion is that if you both agree and that is what you really want to do, fine. I warn them and I will warn you however, that in most of the couples that I have counseled, they start off watching it together and eventually the wife will get tired of doing so and will ask the husband to stop looking at it. He will look at her like she is crazy. "Stop watching porn? Have you lost your mind?" he shouts back. He enjoys the visual stimulation and is probably excited and triggered by some internal fantasy or theme that has developed. She is starting to feel insecure, thinking that maybe he is more into the women on the computer or television than he is into her. She starts to compare herself to these women and likely comes out short every time. These women are models, actresses and are paid good money to look great and to have what appears to the viewer at least, as perfect sex. The husband may even be looking at the video wondering why his wife can't look like the women in the video. He starts thinking that she is defective and that he got the raw end of the deal in this marriage. He may also see the women in the video perform sexual acts that his wife won't do or is not as proficient at. Keep in mind, it is a movie; it isn't necessarily real. These women are also professionals and get paid good money to be good at having sex. Objectification and comparison are a disastrous combination.

Couples would be wise to avoid watching pornography all together. I have had men say, "the videos are educational and that is how I learn new things." There may be a small educational component, but I am extremely skeptical. The best way to learn how to please your wife is for the two of you to get naked, jump in bed, and play with one another until you figure things out. When that occurs, play some more and figure something else out. When that happens, play some more...well you get the idea.

Email and Social Media

I have seen increasing amounts of couples get in arguments over e-mails and messages on social media sites. I had a wife call me one night in tears because she found messages that her deployed military husband had just posted to another woman on Face Book. If you send an e-mail, a text message, or post a message on a social media site, it is there for the world to see – and it will come back to bite you. If you don't believe me, just look at the news and the stories of politicians, sports stars, and other public figures that have lost their careers, their livelihood, and their families as a result of these types of actions.

I recommend that you don't e-mail anyone of the opposite sex unless it is someone you and your spouse both know and you tell him or her that you are doing so ahead of time and you let them read the e-mail afterwards if they desire. This will eliminate any mistrust, secrecy, or ambiguity regarding the behavior and the relationship you have with the person you are corresponding with. I further recommend that you do not keep in contact with old girlfriends or boyfriends. These old friends and lovers have a way of becoming new lovers and affair partners. Avoid the drama; avoid the temptation and just steer clear.

It will be better in the long run for all concerned. Finally, social media is out of control. I personally do not do social media currently, but intend to in the near future for business purposes. I just don't have the time or desire to spend the amount of extra time online that keeping up with others might possibly require. I also think that for some, the temptation can be too great and it is like "playing with fire."

I heard a person once say that he believed that married couples should not have individual profiles of pages, but instead, should maintain a couple or family page. That makes a lot of sense to me. By doing this, everything is out in the open for both partners to see and everyone that pulls up the page will see that you and your spouse are in a committed relationship. I don't see a down side to this, unless hooking up or corresponding with someone behind your spouse's back is really your intent.

I feel that married individuals who stay in contact with other men or women are simply trying to play both sides. They lack confidence in themselves and are insecure in their relationships. They want to see what else is out there or what they can get away with – without losing what they already have. They want the best of both worlds – married and single. It is also about power and control. This person may want to prove that he or she can call the shots; that he or she can have what they want, when they want, and that others will submit or defer to them. This is an attitude of entitlement, with the person believing that they deserve to have the affection and benefits of being with more than one person. They may even feel sorry for one or both of these other individuals, believing that these individuals will somehow be happier or better off by being in a relationship with him or her. Much of what I have been speaking about seems to pertain mostly to men, but may apply to some women as well. There is documented research showing that the gender attitudes and roles regarding sexuality are shifting. This, in part, accounts for why so many more women are viewing pornography than used to.

Concluding Thoughts

As you can see by the vast discussion in this chapter, infidelity can take many different shapes and sizes. This is why couples need to define infidelity for themselves and figure out what specific behaviors are permissible and which aren't. Couples need to be transparent and operate in such a way that everything is out in the open with no secrets. Do not assume that what you are not saying to each other is not important. These unsaid things can be critical and can be just as hurtful as any other type of intentional secret. In the military, we are taught to ask ourselves three important questions: "what do I know?" "Who else needs to know?" "Have I told them?" The answer to the second question is obvious in this case – your spouse. The first question is a little more difficult. I would just simply say that if you have any doubt – tell them. Better that you share something of little significance than to keep something to yourself that might be considered a big deal. The third question is also easy – yes or no. If the response is no, then you need to do it – sooner as opposed to later.

When it comes to relationships and infidelity, we can get ourselves into a lot of trouble in a hurry. We need to be alert for personal and relational vulnerabilities, temptations, and situations that could lead to problems. We should apply a risk assessment model and not engage in any behavior where the potential cost is just too high. This might mean refusing to go to lunch with a co-worker, working late with someone, traveling out of town together, going to a particular bachelor party, or accepting someone as a friend on *Face Book*. We need to be smart and ask ourselves if what we are doing or are about to do is something that we would be comfortable doing with our spouse present. If the answer is no, then we need to stop and talk to our spouse about it because we are now transitioning into the world of secrecy and deceit.

Exercise

Questions for Consideration: Answer each question to the best of your ability, being as thorough as possible in your response.

1. Which of the specific categories of infidelity have been most problematic for you and your spouse or which potentially cause you the most concern in the future and why?

2. What are your most specific risk factors with regards to infidelity from the perspective of opportunity and vulnerability?

3. Taking into consideration those things that were discussed in this chapter, what have you found most helpful and why? How might having an understanding of the various ways in which infidelity can occur help you in your relationship today?

CHAPTER THREE

Why Infidelity Occurs

There are many reasons why men and women cheat. The research results on the exact number of couples that do cheat are very inconsistent, but some recent numbers put it as high as 40% for women and 60% for men. Why men and women cheat is a very complex question and will require us to examine factors pertaining to both the individual and to the relationship. In some cases there may not be an identifiable reason and in others, there will be several.

Individual Factors

Infidelity does not take place in a vacuum; there are reasons why it occurs. The first place we need to look is at personal or individual reasons. The first of these is one that we will discuss at length in the next chapter – the presence of a sexual addiction. When a person is addicted to sex, they think about it all the time; it controls their thoughts, feelings, and actions. This person will be controlled by the addiction, and ultimately by sex. Like other addictions, it is treatable, but not curable. The person will have to make some changes in an effort to live a healthier, more productive life. The important point with this category of individual however, is that there is a medical reason for the behavior and it will ultimately require treatment and other forms of professional help to correct.

Infidelity as a Means to Fill a Void or to Escape

Infidelity is often times a way of escaping. You may be asking yourself "What is so bad that the person needs an escape or what is he or she trying to escape from?" Common things that I hear people mention with regards to escaping include: stress related to work, relationships, and finances; as well as pressure to provide, care for, or be more involved in family roles and functions; and feelings of unhappiness or a life that lacks overall meaning and purpose. In other words, the person is trying to use an affair, sex, or an emotional relationship as a way to numb themselves or to feel joy. It is similar to the person who drinks or uses drugs to get a buzz or achieve a high in an effort to forget or just feel better.

A person that is acting out for these reasons is simply trying to fill a void. They are using the behavior as a way to self-medicate or self-soothe. They have trained their brain to find pleasure or satisfaction from these behaviors and the brain will subsequently signal the rest of the body to engage accordingly in an attempt to feel a sense of normality. This level of normality subsequently becomes the "new normal" that the individual now needs to feel satisfied or "right." The problem is that this behavior is destructive and any pleasure derived from the behavior usually lasts only a very short while. The real solution is to look for and engage in healthy and positive ways to deal with the underlying stressors and issues that are driving or contributing to the problematic behavior.

In most cases however, the person feels so overwhelmed, helpless, and hopeless that he or she doesn't know what to do or where to turn for help. This is where counseling can be extremely helpful if the person will go. It is also the reason why preventative measures are so critical. Individuals need to find ways to achieve balance in their lives and to effectively reduce and deal with stress. It is about becoming more resilient, which I believe happens by making healthy choices and having appropriate outlets. In other words, we need to have hobbies and interests; we need to take care of ourselves physically; and we need to establish meaningful relationships with the right people in our lives. Additionally, we need to find those things that give our life meaning and purpose. This includes having a good relationship with God, having a career or life role that gives our life purpose, and having people in our daily life that love and care about us. If we are taking care of ourselves physically, emotionally, and spiritually, we will be happier and more resilient and will likely not need an affair to fill a void.

Infidelity in Response to Feelings of Loneliness or Neglect

I have had many married men and women who have had affairs tell me that what they discovered and didn't realize at the time of the affair is that they simply felt lonely, unloved, unappreciated, and/or neglected. These feelings can result from many relational factors and situations. For example, many of the men that I have counseled for infidelity state that the affair or behavior occurred when their wife was pregnant or shortly after the baby was born. Consider this scenario if you will: The wife gets pregnant and becomes less sexual and affectionate with her husband.

She isn't feeling well physically and does not like how the extra weight is making her look. She does not feel attractive or sexy. Her self-esteem is being lowered as a result. She is also distracted by preparations for the baby and the long list of extra tasks that need to be accomplished. She may also be struggling with the impact the pregnancy and impending birth will have on her career. Her focus has shifted from her husband and the relationship to the baby and certain key events in support of the upcoming birth. He feels pushed away or neglected, but may not even recognize this fact.

Following the birth of the baby, the mother is recovering physically and is totally invested in the care and nurturing of the child – sometimes at the expense of caring for her husband. He continues to feel neglected, abandoned, and alone. Then one day a beautiful co-worker strikes up a conversation and seems to take an active interest in him and in his life. They have lunch, start spending more time together, and before long, they are involved in an all-out physical and emotional affair. Keep in mind however, a woman does not need to get pregnant or have a baby for the husband to feel neglected and lonely. These feelings can result from simply not spending enough time together, and either one can end up feeling this way. Women typically want a husband that will devote time and energy to them and to the relationship. They want husbands that will hold a meaningful conversation with them and that will share their feelings. Men want a wife who will respect them, show them affection and attention, and who will care for and support them. When men and women become preoccupied with other things (e.g., work, school, kids, clubs, hobbies, and friends), the other person is very susceptible to an affair. The most obvious types of infidelity stemming from these feelings include: physical affairs; chatting online; texting and/or sexting; spending time with and getting emotionally close to co-workers and friends of the opposite sex; and possibly going to interactive porn sites, strip clubs, or adult book stores. This person is using the infidelity as a means to feel connected and of value.

This type of infidelity is likely to occur in relationships in which one or both partners have very demanding careers, where one or both travel a lot for work or pleasure, where there is little to no emotional bonding or connection, and where they fail to communicate in a way that is fulfilling. A couple experiencing an affair for these reasons will likely benefit greatly from couple and family counseling.

Infidelity Resulting from not being Attracted to or Interested in their Spouse

I have had many individuals (usually, but not always men) say that they just don't consider their spouse to be attractive any more. This may be partially the result of age or having children, but the husband will say he just doesn't find her attractive or sexy like he used to. They may feel that their wife doesn't put any effort into her appearance or has become lazy with regards to dressing and looking nice. Both men and women complain about this last point and it can result in the perception that the other person just doesn't care or love them enough to put forth the necessary or desired effort. Women may not take the time or put forth the effort to put on make-up, wear sexy or attractive clothing, or put on their most intimate lingerie.

Men may come across as not caring about their personal hygiene and may spend much of their time at home unshaven; needing a shower; or wearing an old t-shirt, jeans, or sweats.

In addition to these personal factors, there may be emotional ones as well. I have had many wives tell me that they just don't feel like they are important to their husband. They don't feel appreciated or loved. What they desire is attention and to feel as though they are the most important person in their husband's life. The husband may want to simply be left alone – for his wife to stop complaining or "nagging" him. There is a cycle that naturally develops around these two positions: The wife feels neglected, unloved, unappreciated, and unimportant. She tries to compensate for this by drawing closer to him, telling him what she needs. He interprets this as nagging or complaining (the message being that he isn't good enough) and subsequently withdraws further from her. This causes her to feel the same emotions as before, just stronger – until she either gives up or they end up in an argument over it. In this example, the husband and wife have become something or someone that is undesirable or unattractive on various levels to the other spouse. It is easy to get from here to the point that someone else looks much better – especially when such an opportunity presents itself.

Infidelity to Gain Validation

One of the dynamics I have seen pertaining to infidelity with many people is that of infidelity connected to the need for validation. Imagine a middle-aged husband (late thirties to fifties). He has a great career, a loving wife, and perhaps even several children. His life is full and he has a lot to be grateful for. In many respects, he is at the top of his game and should be enjoying life. He also leads a very hectic, challenging, and at times chaotic life with many different responsibilities. On a more personal and self-reflective level he is also starting to recognize that he is getting older and as a result, may be questioning his own value and desirability. In other words, he may not feel that he would appeal to younger, more beautiful women.

You may be thinking "why would he care about being desirable or having a younger woman be attracted to him? After all, he has a wife, children, and career." The issue is that we don't want to be seen as getting older or losing the ability to influence and attract people. As a result of this vulnerability, this man is going to be extremely susceptible to the attention and advances of a younger, attractive, and desirable woman. It could be a work or social situation, or even an acquaintance he meets at the airport or some other neutral location. In other words, he could be easily seduced into an affair (short or long-term).

This is the vulnerability that escorts are typically seeking to fulfill and why they make so much money doing it. Picture a young, incredibly beautiful woman offering this man her companionship and ultimately her body. She gives him a "girlfriend experience" consisting of conversation, exquisite dress and makeup to enhance her natural beauty, and may even entice him further by modeling sexy lingerie. In his mind, he sees a woman that would never be with him, but she is giving him the full illusion that she does. She reaffirms and validates his worth as a man and as a lover. She is his fantasy present in reality. It doesn't matter that he is paying her. The monetary exchange is downplayed and serves as nothing but a minimal distraction from the fantasy and the overall experience.

Like men, women are also susceptible to these types of affairs. The general dynamic is the same, but for the woman, it is likely to come at a point after she has had children possibly even after menopause or at a time when she is questioning her worth. She may not have a career outside the home and as the children become fully grown and move out, she may start to question what she has to offer as a woman. Her husband may be preoccupied with other things and she may also feel neglected or abandoned - similar to feelings discussed in an earlier section. She may feel that her husband does not find her attractive and sexy like he once did so she essentially settles for the current situation, trying to simply accept where she is in life. That changes however, when and if someone shows her attention and begins to validate her beauty, charm and identity as a woman. This woman could be easily seduced into an affair relationship. Unlike men who are more likely to engage in a shorter sexual affair, women may seek the stronger emotional connection and subsequently, engage in a longer relationship.

Affairs like that just described oftentimes lead to the husband or wife leaving their spouse for someone else they met on or offline. It may be surprising to many of us to learn that a friend has left their spouse to fly to another state to be with someone they met on the internet. It sounds crazy, yet it is happening every day. This happened to a friend of my brother years ago. They had been married just two or three years. They had a young child and he was working long hours in his business. She met a man online and a couple months later, left her husband and child, traveling more than a thousand miles, to be with a man she had never actually met. It sounds absurd, but it happens – for exactly the reasons discussed.

An even more extreme example was a woman I counseled who had met a man online who happened to live in a middle-eastern country. She and her husband had been married about eight years and they had two children together. As I recall, she also had a child from a previous marriage. She was referred to me by a colleague because she was contemplating leaving her husband and children to be with this man in another country. What made it worse was that this man was very emotionally abusive in his e-mails and chats with her and would become enraged when she took too long to respond. He even told her that he would beat her and rape her if necessary when she eventually arrived. Even given this information, she was still considering going. She felt that she no longer loved her husband and that this man she met online really "understood" her. Fortunately, she did not go and she and her husband started going to couple counseling. They are both doing much better and the marriage is on a new path. It scares me however, to think about how close she came to losing everything – possibly even her life.

Relational Factors

In addition to individual factors that contribute to infidelity, there are also many types of relational factors. Some researchers and relationship experts contend that affairs are simply the symptom of problems in the marriage or relationship. There is no disputing this fact, but that is also a very simplistic way of conceptualizing the affair process. I am of the belief that *both* individual *and* relational factors contribute to infidelity. The individual factors are significant, but when there are problems in the primary relationship, appropriate measures are not available to prevent the affair, and the couple does not have the necessary tools to adequately deal with the affair and to mitigate or minimize the effects.

Not Spending Time Together

Most of the couples that I have counseled in which an affair occurred agreed that they felt lonely and neglected by their spouse prior to having the affair. They said the primary reason was that they did not spend time together as a couple. Instead, they were preoccupied with work, school, chores, children, hobbies, friends, extended family, and a host of other things that could and do distract couples from each other and from the most important relationship in the home and in their lives – the marriage.

Couples need to spend quality time together nurturing the relationship and keeping the passion alive. Date nights are important and should be a standard practice – whether or not the couple has kids at home or not. I recommend that couples go out together on a date at least once a week. If that simply is not possible, then go out at least every other week. Dates with other couples can be good once in a while, but as a rule, it should be about spending time with each other. If this idea scares you for some reason or you would rather watch reruns on television, then we have a problem.

Some couples mistakenly believe that spending time together as a family and with the kids is the same as a date with your spouse. This simply is not the case. You need a break from the kids and the kids need a break from you. It will be good for all concerned. You are going to now tell me that it is difficult finding a babysitter and that they are expensive. These are valid points. Talk to your friends and neighbors; who do they use for babysitting? Ask around at work, church, and other social settings. One great way to save money on babysitting is to trade these services with another couple. In other words, take turns watching each other's children. The two families may become great friends in the process.

I often have couples tell me they can't afford to go out. You don't have to spend a lot of money to enjoy time together. Go places where you can simply spend time talking or enjoying an activity. Many places have free concerts in the summer. Have a picnic at the park. Spend an afternoon or evening at the beach. Go for a nice bike ride. Take a day trip on a motorcycle or drive someplace for the day. The key is to spend time together talking, connecting, and getting to know each other better. I had a couple once tell me that they go on weekly date nights, but they go a step further by taking turns planning the event. They make it more romantic and somewhat of a mystery as well by only giving the other person enough information so they know what to wear and when to be ready. This can be exciting and your spouse might really enjoy the anticipation, element of surprise, and romance.

I am of the opinion that couples who spend consistent time together will continue to appreciate each other more and will fall further in love with one another throughout the duration of the marriage. This will serve as a major deterrence for the affair and will strengthen the couple so that they will be better prepared to effectively deal with the affair should one occur. It therefore serves as both a preventive measure and as a mitigating factor. Many couples, by not spending time together, are making an affair more likely to occur and they are depriving themselves of the tools and skills necessary to recover from the affair should one occur. It only makes sense that couples should want to spend time together. To do so however, they must make their relationship a priority.

Communication Problems

Another major relational factor contributing to affairs is difficulty communicating in a real and meaningful way. Many couples spend very little time talking and when they do, it is very superficial and void of any real emotion or intimacy. Couples need to communicate in such a way that they feel understood and supported. They need to feel that their spouse cares about them and the challenges they are going through in their lives. They need to connect during joyous or happy times, as well as in times of disappointment and frustration. Couples need to communicate in such a way that they feel each other's pain and heartache. This will communicate empathy and genuine concern. As a result, the individual will not feel alone, neglected, or abandoned. They will feel connected to their spouse in a positive and intimate way. Couples also need to share in each other's victories and continue to encourage one another. We should be our spouse's greatest cheerleader and be willing and ready to sing their praises. Get excited about each other's accomplishments and show them that you are on their team.

You are probably thinking, "That all sounds good, but how do I actually accomplish this?" The key is connection and it takes practice. Men, more often than women, will have difficulty with this. Men are taught not to show emotion and that emotion is a sign of weakness. They then get married and their wife, as well as some book that their wife just bought says to show emotion. Not so fast. For people to share emotion, they must feel safe enough to do so. They can't feel as though they will be judged or criticized because of what they are about to share. This is a vulnerable place to be and with it comes a lack of comfort and stability. There is a risk involved. Therefore, wives may need to encourage their husbands to take the risk of sharing and being vulnerable. It takes time, patience, and a lot of positive reinforcement.

Other factors to consider in this communication process are the mechanics and practical issues surrounding the communication itself. First, set time aside and make this a priority. Like going to the gym, if you don't set time aside and make it part of your routine, you won't do it. Meaningful couple communication does not have to take a long time. Twenty or thirty minutes can make a significant difference. Once you start talking to each other and really engage on an emotional and intimate level you won't want to stop. Remember what it was like going out together in the beginning of your dating relationship, sitting in the car or on the porch swing talking for hours? That is what this will feel like again. You will connect in ways and on a level that you haven't for quite some time. One of the most difficult, yet critical pieces to this process is to free yourself of distractions. This means you need to put away the cell phone, ignore or silence the home phone, make sure the kids are tucked in or are away somewhere, take care of the dogs and cats, turn off the computer and the television and go someplace comfortable where you can look at each other while you are speaking, and more importantly - listening.

Another aspect of the mechanical process is to apply good communication skills. There are many books on this subject available at the library, local bookstores, and online. The most important part however, as highlighted in the last paragraph is to listen. Stop worrying about what you are going to say and just listen to your partner. Speak using I statements. For example, "I feel appreciated when you compliment me on my cooking. It makes me feel really good." Reflect back or summarize what you hear the person saying. Continuing the example, "My complimenting you makes you feel appreciated. I do appreciate you and want to show you how much I love you so I will try to do this more." Try to use feeling words so that you can connect on a deeper level. The best formula or method for doing this is to simply say, "I feel _____ when _____." The challenge is not to blame the other person. Speak to the actions not the person. For example, don't say, "I feel worthless because you are a lousy husband and are always ignoring me." Instead, say "I love spending time with you and connecting with you. When you watch television or play videogames, I sometimes feel ignored and even worthless. It makes me think you don't want to spend time with me." Notice the specificity level in describing the behavior, as well as the relatively small shift in focus and likely lowered resistance from the spouse when hearing this.

Non-verbal behaviors account for about 80% of communication so keep in mind that it is not just what you say, but how you say it. Watch the non-verbal behaviors and make sure they are consistent with your words and the intended message. If you slow the process down and carefully apply these simple ideas, your communication will greatly improve.

It is important to keep in mind that as couples communicate in healthier ways, their relationships will become stronger and the intimacy will increase. As this happens, couples will be more deeply attracted to one another which will make an affair less likely to occur. This is because the feelings of neglect, abandonment, and loneliness will dissipate to manageable or even non-existent levels. As stated earlier, if an affair was to occur with this healthy level of communication present in the relationship, they would be able to reach out to one another emotionally and would have a much better chance of recovering from the infidelity if it actually occurred in the first place.

Not Dealing with Problems in the Relationship

Connected to the previous two issues are situations in which couples are not dealing with the relational problems that exist in the marriage. By not dealing with or possibly even ignoring these issues, the couple allows tension to build which can lend itself to frustration, bitterness, and resentment. As this happens, a wall is built between the husband and wife, making it virtually impossible for them to communicate and connect. They will likely make snide comments towards one another, saying hurtful things to one another, engaging in passive-aggressive behaviors, and even escalating into arguments and physical fights. As the couple continues to act in this manner, one or both partners will eventually withdraw from the situation. This is the point at which they may seek comfort from another person; even looking for a new partner – someone that can offer validation, affection, appreciation, attention, and nurturance. Conditions are now ripe for an affair to occur because other people will look particularly attractive on an emotional, if not physical level.

In order to minimize the chances of a situation such as this occurring, it is important that couples communicate effectively so that they can work through issues as they develop. They need to have regular conversations, couple and family meetings, and strategize plans for dealing with the issues that come up in the relationship. This is a proactive approach and is one that can have very positive effects. The couple needs to work on establishing a deeper level of intimacy so that they can each feel safe in bringing up difficult topics, seeking support from their spouse, and turning towards them in time of deepest need. If the difficult issues or topics are left unattended, they will only fester like a bad infection until the point at which the relationship becomes visibly affected. If this continues, the end result can be incapacitation or in the marriage – divorce.

Exercise

Questions for Consideration: Answer each question to the best of your ability, being as thorough as possible in your response.

1. Describe the individual factors that most likely contributed to the affair in your marital relationship?

2. Describe the relational factors that contributed to an affair in your marital relationship.

3. Taking into consideration those things that were discussed in this chapter, what have you found most helpful and why? How might having an understanding of why people cheat help you in your relationship today?

CHAPTER FOUR

When Infidelity Becomes Compulsive

What does Compulsive Sex Look Like?

A while back, I was counseling a couple that had been married slightly more than thirty years. They had come to see me as a result of his sexual acting out. More specifically, his wife had recently discovered that he was having an affair and that he had been having affairs for almost thirty years. You are probably wondering how come it took her so long to discover these affairs, especially given the fact that she is a very intelligent woman. She told me that during this time she would notice things that seemed unusual; she would even ask her husband about them and he would always have a reasonable explanation. She did not have any reason not to trust him so she bought into whatever excuse, lie, or story he happened to have. When the truth finally came out however, she remarked that at least now she knew that she hadn't been imagining things and feeling like she was going crazy. In that moment, there was actually a small sense of relief.

This is just one of many cases I have personally seen of infidelity rooted in sexual addiction. It is estimated that one in ten Americans suffer from sexual addiction. I personally believe that number may be low and I certainly feel that the percentage of sex addicts is higher among particular populations such as military service members and college students. It is important to recognize however, that sexual addiction does not discriminate on the basis of age, race, gender, or religion. In other words, it is an equal opportunity disease. I say disease because I adhere to the guidance of the American Medical Association in their philosophy that addiction, regardless of specific type, is a disease and as such, follows a discernable pattern of progression.

Assessment and Diagnosis

It is also worth noting at this point that although clinicians essentially agree that sexual addiction exists, there is not currently a diagnosis for it in the Diagnostic and Statistical Manual of Mental Disorders (DSM-IV TR, 2000) published by the American Psychiatric Association. Sexual addiction may be placed in the next revision, but that has not been confirmed. In making a preliminary or situational diagnosis for sexual addiction, most therapists use the same criteria as they would for chemical dependency and simply substitute the specific behavior(s) involved. Therefore, a formal diagnosis would include the following:

1. Tolerance

2. Withdrawal

3. Unsuccessful attempts to cut back or quit

4. Engaging in the behavior more often or for longer amounts of time than intended

5. Excessive time preparing to engage in the behavior or recovering from it

6. Continuing the behavior despite physical or psychological consequences

7. Impaired social or occupational functioning as a result of engaging in the behavior

Assessment

Information to be used in making a clinical decision regarding the presence of sexual addiction can be obtained through a clinical interview with a therapist as well as utilizing assessment instruments such as the Sexual Addiction Screening Test (SAST) available for public use on the website, www.sexhelp.com. The SAST is a 45 question true/false instrument that measures the presence of sexual addiction based on a comparison of responses to an experimental group consisting of sex addicts treated in both outpatient and inpatient facilities. This instrument can be completed in approximately 10-15 minutes. There are versions of this instrument available for women, as well as gay/lesbian clients on the same website.

Diagnostic Criteria

I had a young Marine that I was counseling individually that was also part of a therapy group I was facilitating for sex addicts. He was addicted to online pornography and his fiancée told him that if they were going to get married, he would have to stop looking at pornography all together. He had been looking at porn since he was a young teenager so he knew this would not be easy, but he had no idea it would be as difficult as it actually turned out to be. He described having physical withdrawal symptoms when he stopped looking at porn. These symptoms included: profuse sweating, inability to concentrate, difficulty sleeping, and shaking. In all of the cases I have had, I only know of about four or five that experienced any noticeable form of physical withdrawal whatsoever.

Tolerance is likely to be another matter entirely. Tolerance is simply a situation where it takes more or increasing amounts of a substance or behavior to have the same effect. Stated differently, a person taking the same amount of a substance or engaging in the same amount or type of behavior over time will feel a diminishing effect. Our brain gets used to the behavior and begins to identify it as the new or desired "norm." When we think of tolerance with alcohol, it is relatively easy to understand that drinking a six pack of beer tonight will have a different effect than it will a month from now (provided I continue to drink on a regular basis). If I want to feel the same effect next month, I will likely have to drink nine or ten beers.

With pornography specifically and sexual addiction in general, the behavior is not measured only in terms of quantity. For example, three hours on the computer looking at porn today will not have the same impact as three hours on the computer looking at porn next month (assuming a regular pattern of engaging in the behavior). As time progresses, individuals will need to be on the computer for longer periods of time or at a higher frequency. They may also respond by escalating to more intense sites or by engaging in riskier behaviors. For example, a person that spends two hours a night, three nights a week looking at pornography depicting couples having sex, may start looking at pornography four hours a night four or five nights a week. He or she may also switch form sites depicting couples to sites depicting group sex; swapping; fetishes; or even sexual scenes involving gay, lesbian, bisexual, and transsexual individuals. The key is not the specific behaviors involved, but the escalation to those of higher risk or that are perceived as being less acceptable by society. In more extreme cases, this escalation can also include illegal behaviors such as child pornography.

I have had a few individuals who were addicted to porn escalate to child pornography even though they did not appear to have a sexual attraction to children. It was the risk that produced the high – not the images themselves. Another client of mine would break into houses in his neighborhood as a teenager for the sole purpose of finding and stealing their porn. He would also drink some of their alcohol and eat some of their food. He described the rush as being associated with the risk of being caught. He even remarked that the biggest rush came when the neighbors would come home while he was still in the house. It is no surprise that his sexual behavior was rooted in risk. He had cheated a lot on his wife in many different ways – all in an effort to see if he could get away with it.

In addition to tolerance and withdrawal previously discussed, individuals suffering from sexual addiction are likely to have tried to cut back or stop several times before. This may be the man who swears he will stop going to strip clubs with friends after work, the husband who has thrown out his porn stash of expensive videos ten times in the last fifteen years, or it may be the wife who keeps recommitting herself to a life of faithfulness, promising to stop sleeping with men she meets at work – only to wake up next to yet another man a few days later.

What typically motivates a sex addict to get help or to seek counseling are the consequences involved with the behavior. These consequences can take many different forms. There may be legal consequences resulting from an arrest for prostitution or solicitation, exhibitionism, voyeurism, or viewing child pornography as just a few examples. I have had clients who had been arrested for exposing themselves at the mall, while walking on a public sidewalk, and even while on a combat deployment to Iraq. Voyeurism, or peeping, has become much more advanced with changes in technology. People no longer need to look inside windows while women undress. They can install and use miniature cameras strategically placed for the optimum effect and record the entire event for later viewing in the security of their home or office. With this shift in technology comes less likelihood of getting caught. Individuals like those just mentioned are seeking help because they are in trouble with the law. They have been arrested or cited and are facing possible jail time, legal fees and fines, and public humiliation. In some situations, this behavior can also involve loss of professional licenses or livelihood such as the case when doctors, nurses, therapists, politicians, and sports celebrities are involved.

Legal problems may be one of the consequences facing those addicted to sex, but there are many others to consider as well. Financial consequences may be a factor. It used to be that in order for a person to access pornography; he or she would have to go to the store and purchase it or buy it through a mail-order distributor. That has changed. Individuals can access pornography online for free. There may be a fee for some types of porn, particularly hard-core or riskier types, but much of it can still be obtained for free. The financial consequences typically result from other types of sexual acting out. I had a Marine tell me that he was spending between $300-400 a week at a local strip club. Although the dancers appreciated it, his wife didn't. I had a senior Officer see me for a sexual addiction that involved paying for sexual dates with escorts. He estimated that he was spending between one and two thousand dollars a month. His wife was unaware of the behavior and the money that he was spending, but he knew it was only a matter of time.

Although I have not had any clients come in stating that they had contracted a sexually transmitted disease (STD) through their sexual acting out, it is definitely possible, and it does happen. In addition to STDs, unwanted pregnancy is a real concern, as are other health risks and issues stemming directly or indirectly from sexual behavior.

Perhaps the most common category of consequences resulting from compulsive sexual behavior or addiction is relational. Nearly all of the people I have treated for sexual addiction have come to me because of the impact the behavior was having on their marriage or other significant relationships. I can't count the number of times a person (typically the husband) has come to me because their spouse has caught them acting out either on or offline. One of the most memorable was a young man about 24 years old who had been referred to me by another therapist who had been treating him for chemical dependency.

During a clinical interview in which we were discussing his sexual behavior, he revealed to me that he was separated from his wife and that she was divorcing him because of his infidelity. He also stated that he was living with a girl-friend. He then told me that he had slept with approximately 285 women in his lifetime thus far and that he had had 57 threesomes. I thought to myself "wow! That seems like a lot." More importantly, I wondered why he was keeping count. At that point came the most significant part of the conversation. He told me that he had never been faithful to any woman and that he didn't think he ever could. He cried as he told me that he loved his wife and wished they could stay married.

One of my very first sex addiction cases was a young man who had come to see me because his wife had caught him on the computer masturbating to images of women performing various sexual acts. He, like many men, told me that he was seeking help because he got caught – not necessarily because he wanted to change his behavior. He also told me that he would not be there had he not been caught, and that he felt it was his wife that had the problem, not him. In his eyes, his wife was the one with the problem because he was "just doing what guys do" and that she should just accept it. After some rapport building and encouragement, I managed to get him to just be open to the idea that some of his behavior was problematic. He did tell me however, that if she was to leave him, he would not come back for counseling. Therapy progressed and he did quite well. Approximately two months after beginning therapy, he said that his therapy was no longer contingent on whether his wife left or not; He liked the person he was becoming and felt that he was on a much better path. This was a milestone event – one indicative of real and significant progress. He was able to recognize the fact that he did have a problem and that he needed help.

Sometimes consequences overlap. This is quite common in the military. I had a young Marine who had come back from a combat deployment to Iraq. He had developed a pretty severe case of combat stress and post traumatic stress disorder (PTSD). He was using sex as a way to escape the feelings and numb the pain associated with the combat experiences. One day, in the middle of the afternoon, while working in an office setting surrounded by both men and women (some of which were civilians) in individualized open cubicles, he accessed pornography on his government work computer and began to masturbate to the images. Several of the women noticed what was happening and went to the supervisor for help. The supervisor immediately intervened and stopped the behavior. The young man was turned over to legal for appropriate disciplinary action. The interesting, and to some extent promising, thing about this case is that the individual ultimately received inpatient therapy designed to deal with the addiction as well as the trauma. He was scheduled to be court-martialed for his actions, but I do not know the outcome. I believe he was able to stay on active duty following treatment. Many people do not receive this level of treatment as it is quite expensive. It is also difficult to get insurance companies and managed health care organizations to authorize such care. His physical and emotional injuries from war, as well as the sexual addiction itself took a significant toll on his marriage. Although they managed to stay together, they experienced significant stress in their marriage and were literally coping one day at a time. This is a great example of a situation in which the addiction had work, relationship, and legal implications. It goes without saying that these behaviors resulted in financial consequences as well.

In addition to consequences, another major factor in the determination of sexual addiction is the concept of having lost control. I often ask people whether they feel that their sexual desire controls them or if they control it. Take the story of Billy (not his real name). Billy came to see me shortly after he returned from a combat deployment to Iraq. He was struggling with sexual addiction consisting of pornography and masturbation. When asked about his sexual history and when he first felt masturbation had become a problem, he indicated that it probably became most noticeable in Iraq. I asked how often he masturbated while over there. I was shocked by his response – nine to ten times a day, possibly more depending on the watch rotation. He said it was worse on watch because of the boredom. This resulted in him spending a great deal of his time on watch (when he was supposed to be providing security) masturbating. This is a good example of not being in control.

What Being Addicted is Like

Being addicted to sex is described by many addicts as the worst addiction a person can have. Even those with severe drug addictions describe sexual addiction as being magnitudes worse. In addition to physically being one of the most devastating and challenging addictions a person can have, sexual addiction is made worse by society and its messages regarding sexuality. Perhaps this short illustration will help: I can walk into a room and say "Hi, I am Mike and I am an alcoholic." People will have an understanding of what that means. Some may greet me and share their own stories of alcoholism and recovery. If I walk in to a room and say "Hi, I am Mike and I am a sex addict" I will likely soon find myself standing alone with everyone else bunched together leering at me. There is a stigma with sexual addiction because people do not understand it. The media pokes fun at the topic and often headlines sensationalize it. Many people also mistakenly correlate sex addiction with pedophilia. It is important for people to understand that a sex addict is not necessarily a sex offender and vice versa. The term "sex offender" is a legal one and means that the person has been found guilty in a court of law for a sexually based crime.

Sex addicts typically have skewed beliefs about men, women, and sex. They were likely taught by other kids, including relatives, about sex. They may also have been sexually abused as a child. Research shows that approximately 84% of sex addicts were sexually abused as children. That number is higher for emotional abuse and nearly as high for physical abuse. Many of the sex addicts I have treated were molested as young children; grew up in detached families in which parents and siblings failed to support, encourage, or , connect with one another; and developed an unhealthy attitude and understanding of human sexuality. Many of these individuals experienced a lack of romantic or dating relationships or were excessively promiscuous, thus learning to connect emotions to sex. Regardless of the path, both groups of individuals experienced difficulty in forming healthy attachments and therefore developed a dysfunctional approach towards love and nurturing.

As the addict learns to look at the world through these flawed lenses of sexual misinformation, they respond in distorted ways. This damaged belief system feeds directly into what some researchers have coined the arousal template. All human beings have an arousal template. It is comprised of our fantasies and the elements of our sexuality and world view that gets us sexually excited or stimulated. The first part is physical and has to do with the physical features that we are most attracted or responsive to. For example, one might be most attracted to a woman's breasts or her legs. It could also be seemingly non-sexual parts such as her face, nose, or hair. There are personality factors that drive our arousal template as well. For example, I may be most attracted to a confident, independent, hard-working woman. The arousal template can include the kind of career or job a person has, what they do for fun, how they smell, and even mannerisms such as the way they sit, stand, smile, and walk. Many of these things become triggers for driving the sexual acting out behavior. An important and necessary point is that these things become sexually linked and therefore produce sexual stimulation – regardless of whether they are sexual in nature or not.

The arousal template drives our fantasies and may be rooted in early trauma or sexual experiences as well. For example, many men who are used to having sex with escorts or prostitutes in hotel rooms will say that just the smell of the room or even certain hotel signs can trigger them towards acting out. Men who have paid for the services of an escort will also say that the ultimate rush is not the sex itself, but rather, the point at which she knocks at the door and he opens the door to greet this beautiful woman – a woman he has only imagined up to this point. Even with escort sites on the internet and menus of girls that are available for men to view, there is still an element of surprise. This moment is the start of the "date" and the beginning of the psychological process in which the escort begins to convince the man that he is very desirable and that any beautiful, attractive, and intelligent woman would be lucky to have him. It is about making him believe that he has what it takes to be desirable to young, beautiful women. This is his fantasy. She isn't really interested in him, but a good escort will convince him that she is.

As the arousal template forms the structure for the fantasy, the person begins to engage in certain ritualistic behaviors. This is essentially the preparation or preliminary behavior connected with acting out. It may involve getting new clothes, lingerie, a faster computer, or even making sure that one's spouse in unavailable or adequately distracted. It is about preparing everything necessary so that the sexual behavior can actually occur. It may also include activities such as searching the phone book or the computer for available escorts during a business trip. Once these preliminary steps are completed, the person engages in the actual compulsive behavior. The behavior is obviously important, but equally important is the resultant impact that the behavior has on the individual and the neurological systems of the brain that deal with stimulation and pleasure. Sexual stimulation affects the dopamine receptor sites and other pleasure sensors in the brain, thus making the person feel like they need to experience the behavior to feel "right" or "normal." This becomes the new norm and the individual will now do all he or she can to experience these heightened states of sexual arousal.

Once the behavior starts, negative consequences soon begin to develop. If the consequences are delayed or for some reason do not appear, the individual will begin thinking that there are no consequences or that he or she is somehow immune from them. For these individuals, reality has yet to set in. Without consequences, individuals will lack motivation for change – including treatment. In my experience it is not so much a matter of *if* the negative consequences of the addictive behavior will appear, but *when*. How bad things need to get before an individual decides to seek help or change is a personal matter however. Each person has a different threshold of pain. Some refer to the point at which a person decides to change as "hitting bottom." I believe this term is misused as people do not always reach the lowest point possible or imaginable before making the decision to get help. The situation just has to be "bad enough." Many addicts that make the decision to embrace recovery say they simply got tired of living with their addiction. This implies a wearing down process.

Recovery from sexual addiction is an extremely difficult journey. There is a lot of shame and guilt surrounding the behaviors involved and the person will likely be found struggling with feelings of failure, disgust, and worthlessness as well. They may feel like they are a mistake as a person and that they negatively impact everyone around them. I have had addicts tell me that they feel "lower than dirt." They may sometimes wonder why they have to live with this disease, as if it is payback for something they did. Some will even question whether God exists, if He is punishing them, and why bad things keep happening.

Defining Recovery

Before moving on in our discussion, it is important to understand what recovery is. As stated earlier, addiction is a disease. It is treatable, but not curable. Once an addict – always an addict; it will not go away. Recovery however, is about making healthy choices that enable the individual to live a life of sobriety. The hope and the goal is that as the person embraces sobriety and recovery, they will experience joy as they reach their full potential in a life that God has designed for them.

Unlike alcohol and drugs where sobriety typically equals abstinence, that is not necessarily the case with sex addiction. Sex is a healthy and important part of a romantic relationship, particularly a marriage. Therefore, complete abstinence would not necessarily be viewed as a good thing – by either partner. It makes sense then that the addict will need to determine what sobriety is in their particular situation. It would be even better if the couple could work together as a team to define sobriety for them, much like their discussion surrounding infidelity in general. I like to use a model consisting of three concentric circles. The inner circle is the smallest of the three and is referred to as the red zone. Although the smallest for illustration purposes, it may actually be the largest in terms of content. This area includes all behaviors that would be considered by either partner to be acting out, off limits, or inappropriate. Examples include things such as viewing pornography, masturbation, sexual contact with anyone other than their spouse, strip clubs, and maybe even spending time alone with someone of the opposite sex. Begin with the things that got you in trouble.

Green zone behaviors comprise the outer circle and include things that the couple deem completely appropriate. This may include sexual activity with each other; using the computer and internet for news, e-mail, and other agreed upon sites; and group luncheons at work where members of the opposite sex may or may not be present. The middle circle is the yellow zone and this is perhaps the most difficult to define. This area includes activities that the couple agrees may be appropriate provided certain safeguards are in place. For example, accessing safe sites (e.g., news, sports, e-mail) on the internet only when someone else is present in the room or in the house, going to the beach or someplace similar where a person might be triggered only if accompanied by certain family members or friends, viewing of particular television shows or movies only if screened prior to watching or if accompanied by the spouse or agreed upon person.

The key to yellow zone behaviors is that these behaviors may be authorized, but only with additional safety considerations. In early recovery, there should be very few yellow zone behaviors as most of these would more appropriately be labeled red zone behaviors. As recovery progresses, the couple should routinely discuss their sobriety plan and see if it requires any changes. This process is important because it identifies behaviors that are unacceptable, while also assessing progress in recovery and changes that may be necessary based on the identification of triggers and changing situations.

Relapse Prevention

Another key element of recovery is to develop a relapse prevention plan. This involves first identifying all applicable triggers. A trigger is a physical or emotional cue that facilitates a craving or seeking response in the brain. For example, a man may be triggered by the site of a beautiful woman on the beach wearing a bikini. Another man may be triggered by a woman at work in a skirt and low cut top. Men are oftentimes triggered by visual cues. It can be a billboard, a picture in a magazine, or a commercial on television. This is in part why companies such as Victoria's Secret are so profitable and put forth tremendous effort in making their ads just right. Women also take time to look and smell their best for this exact reason. They want people (particularly the men in their life) to notice how nice they look. These things speak to the arousal template and men's fixation on visual stimulation. Men are typically quite obvious in their response (e.g., the double take, staring at women as they walk by, or glaring at a woman's cleavage).

Women can be visually stimulated as well. They will typically notice men who have a muscular and somewhat rugged appearance and may be subsequently triggered by this type of look. On the other hand, they may be triggered by the site of a man in a suit, possibly linking attraction with perceived success and wealth. There is research showing that women are attracted to men that can provide stability and security. If they are physically attractive then that is even better.

In addition to physical triggers, I find that virtually all sex addicts are triggered emotionally as well as physically. These typically go unnoticed however, and do not get the attention they deserve in treatment. These triggers are oftentimes stronger and more pervasive in their impact upon the person and the addiction. Emotional triggers typically involve such feelings as boredom, loneliness, powerlessness, and entitlement. These triggers therefore have a significant psychological dimension. For example, many sex addicts will act out when they are bored. Therefore, being home alone, bored, with access to a computer may not be a good thing. A businessman who travels a lot may be triggered by both boredom and loneliness while sitting alone in his hotel room, debating whether or not to seek the companionship of an escort. Regardless of whether or not he acts out, he has already been emotionally triggered. He is thinking about it as he engages in fantasy. The relapse process has started and he is already on a slippery slope.

I had a client once tell me that he would get on the computer and look at porn (sometimes masturbating as well) when he and his wife would have an argument. This was his way of getting even with her. He would not hide the behavior, thus resulting in her almost always observing him doing it. This would upset her even more and the fight would continue to escalate. In this case, the individual's acting out behavior was fueled by his anger towards his wife and a subsequent need for power. He used porn as leverage to gain an upper hand or restore a balance of power following an argument.

Once the triggers are identified, the individual must develop a plan for sobriety that accounts for each of the specific triggers. This plan can include avoiding the trigger all together; but in most cases, will serve to minimize the exposure to a limited or lower amount. For example, a man may be triggered every time he drives by a strip club or a particular hotel in town. He may be able to plan his routes to avoid these establishments, but it is unlikely that he can avoid every hotel of that brand or every strip club. Therefore, if it can be avoided – do so. This would be considered an easy day. If it can't be avoided then the person needs to take additional action in order to minimize the impact of the trigger upon the individual's recovery. I tell people that they need to run as fast and as far from these triggers and the resultant behaviors as possible. In other words, do whatever it takes to remain sober.

Relapse prevention can seem simplistic at times, but it is these specific actions that can keep the person sober. For example, an addict should always have the telephone numbers of five people that he or she can call at anytime if he or she is feeling triggered. These will be people also in recovery, typically people they meet in group. If they are driving down the street and see a sign for a strip club that triggers them for example, they should immediately start dialing those numbers until they reach one of the individuals who can then talk them through the difficult situation. Taking action like this will give them strength to get through the situation as opposed to thinking about the sign, possibly turning around, and ultimately going to the strip club after convincing themselves that it won't hurt anyone, that they deserve it, or that they will only stay for thirty minutes. These forms of rationalization will not further the cause of recovery and will likely lead to relapse. The person should also call their sponsor and attend a twelve-step meeting as soon as possible. The addict needs to realize that they are powerless over their addiction and do everything possible to stay sober. The relapse prevention plan should be detailed in writing and should become second nature – something the person can instinctively do without thinking about it. By the time you start thinking, it may be too late.

Elements of Recovery

In addition to a relapse prevention plan, recovery involves certain key elements. I like to conceptualize recovery as a large tool bag that each person designs in a unique and personal way. The tools contained in the bag are hand selected based on the experiences and needs of the individual. There are no right or wrong tools to be included in the bag as long as they work to help keep the individual sober and promote a generally healthy lifestyle.

The first tool that should be considered is that of a therapist for individual and/or group counseling. The therapist should be someone who understands and is trained in sexual addiction. The International Institute for Trauma and Addiction Professionals (IITAP) maintains a listing of these therapists on their website, www. iitap.com. Another website that contains a listing of therapists is the Society for the Advancement of Sexual Health (SASH). Their website address is www.sash.net. Both of these listings can be searched by name and location. The therapist will help the person develop a recovery plan, will be a source of accountability, and will help the individual develop a deeper understanding of the personal and/ or psychodynamic factors contributing to the addiction. They also serve as a coach, offering encouragement and feedback along the way.

Individual counseling is important for identifying, understanding, and dealing with both intrapersonal and interpersonal factors affecting the addiction. It is also important that the person become a member of a therapeutic group. These groups typically meet once per week for 1-2 hours. These groups offer the individual a broader sense of accountability and encouragement, while also helping the individual to realize that he or she is not alone, that many others share similar stories, and that there is hope in recovery. They also learn recovery tools from those that have been there. They can learn what has worked and what hasn't worked for others. Groups promote true healing as members communicate, support one another, and complete therapeutic tasks.

Another key recovery tool is twelve-step groups. Like Alcoholic Anonymous (AA) for alcoholics and Narcotics Anonymous (NA) for drug addicts, sex addicts can also attend a twelve-step group. The specific type of group differs depending on geographical location. For example, Sexaholics Anonymous (SA) is located primarily on the west coast. Sex Addicts Anonymous (SAA) is located primarily on the east coast. There are also Recovering Couples Anonymous (RCA) which caters to the needs of couples, and Sex and Love Addicts Anonymous (SLAA) which caters primarily to gay, lesbian, and bisexual individuals. Each of these groups serves as a source of support for those suffering from sexual addiction. They do not cost anything and are located in many cities and towns across America. These groups maintain a spiritual emphasis by focusing on a higher power. Early in recovery, I recommend that addicts try to attend at least 3-5 meetings per week. Ideally, it is preferred that the person try to attend ninety meetings in ninety days if at all possible. It is best if these are sex addiction meetings, but AA and/or NA meetings are acceptable as a less preferred option when SA type meetings are unavailable.

From the support group, individual addicts should find a sponsor. This individual serves to some degree as an addiction coach or mentor. They help the individual understand the addiction process, the key steps to recovery, and help them develop and apply a relapse prevention plan as appropriate. The sponsor is a person that the individual will ultimately develop and maintain a very close relationship with. They are the first person the addict should contact when things get difficult and the addict should feel comfortable enough with this individual to bounce ideas or thoughts off of without any fear of retribution or criticism. The sponsor will help the person stay sober and keep their recovery on the right track. They are the voice of experience. "They have been there, done that, and got the shirt to prove it." Early in recovery, an addict should be "checking-in" with his or her sponsor every day. They should also be completing tasks as assigned by the sponsor, including step work. When I have had clients relapse (regardless of the type of addiction), I typically discover that they have not been attending meetings or working with their sponsor on a regular basis. Those that do are much more successful in their recovery.

Sex addiction obviously impacts the marriage and the family. As a marriage and family therapist myself, I am a strong advocate of marital and/or family counseling. I personally feel that couple counseling when sex addiction is present is critically important to the overall recovery process. The difficult question is when is the right time? Once the addict begins recovery and is engaging the addiction in a positive way, then couple counseling, in my opinion, is appropriate. I have heard some say that they should wait a year before working on the relationship. I don't think that waiting that long is reasonable and I don't feel that most marriages would last the year. When I work with couples, I like to make sure it is part of the overall plan, just as individual counseling for the addict, individual counseling for the spouse, and group counseling for either and/or both spouses may be. I typically see the addict weekly. I will also see the couple about twice a month and may even see the spouse twice a month as well. If there are any perceptions of bias or alignment issues with the couple, I will attempt to refer the spouse and/or the couple as appropriate.

The problem I have encountered is that finding a therapist knowledgeable in sex addiction is very difficult. There simply just are not enough therapists with the necessary training and experience. Couple counseling focuses on issues relating to the marriage, but will be heavily influenced by the addiction and compulsive sexual behavior. This will include how the addiction has impacted the marriage, as well as how problems in the marriage may be contributing to the addiction. The addiction and marital relationship can be conceptualized as a system in which both parts impact one another in various ways.

Another aspect of the addiction recovery process is treating the spouse. Men and women who have an addictive spouse often enable the behavior. In so doing, they earn the title, enabler. They may also be so focused on the spouse and his or her recovery that they become co-dependent themselves. This could be a wife who discovered her husband's addiction and has since devoted all of her time to checking up on him, verifying that what he says and does is accurate, and making sure that he is not acting out. The most common example of this type of behavior is the wife who compulsively checks her husband's cell phone, e-mail, and social media looking for messages, pictures, and hidden accounts. As mentioned in an earlier chapter, I once had a male client that was struggling with an online pornography addiction, but his wife was played a critical role by continuing to enable the behavior. Ironically, despite his wife's objections to his computer and internet activities, she served him dinner in the living room at the computer and even permitted him to sleep underneath the computer table on a somewhat regular basis. This would be considered the epitome of enabling behavior and is something that simply should not be occurring. The spouse in situations such as these would benefit greatly from counseling.

One of the issues that couples recovering from addiction struggle with is trust. Assume for a minute that it is the husband that is the addict. Although women can and oftentimes are addicted, it is more common for the man. When the idea of sexual addiction is first presented to the wife, she will likely have a huge problem with it, feeling that it is just a convenient way of justifying the behavior. The other part of this is the fact that the trust in the relationship has been completely eliminated. He will need to become an "open book;" to become completely transparent. He will need to tell her exactly what he is doing and why. He must live up to his word at all times and be completely honest in everything he does. If he says he will be home at a certain time, he better be there. If not, he better let her know ahead of time and have a good reason. She may check his e-mails and cell phone. Although this is not necessarily healthy behavior, she may need the security of it in the early stages of recovery. What seems to get most people in trouble at this stage is not what is said, but rather what is left out. The small details that they did not realize were important become critical.

The focus of the counseling for the spouse should be on them individually and how the addiction has impacted them as a person. The focus should not and must not become the addict or even the marital relationship. Those things overlap and need to be discussed at times, but they should not become the focus. When a wife catches her husband acting out sexually, she will typically ask questions such as these immediately or very soon after:

1. What is wrong with me?

2. Am I not pretty enough?

3. Am I not sexy enough?

4. Am I not good enough in bed?

The focus for her becomes herself and the perceived apparent defect that she feels obviously must exist. The reality of the situation however, is that the addiction has little to nothing to do with her. She is usually just a victim in the situation. It is about him and may not even be about sex. Sex is just the behavior through which the addiction manifests itself. The wife needs counseling to deal with self-esteem issues, forgiveness, understanding the science and psychology of addiction, co-dependency issues, identifying resources, systemic or family effects, learning to trust again, and what this all means for the marriage and the family. In an ideal situation, three separate therapists will be involved, one for the addict, another for the spouse, and yet another for the couple. These therapists should obtain written consent from the clients to communicate and share ideas amongst themselves regarding the case and proper care and treatment.

How Long Should Treatment Take?

Some experts in the field of sex addiction believe that therapy should last 2-3 years, possibly longer. I have seen much more rapid success, with addicts experiencing a significant amount of growth and healing in less than a year. A lot will depend on the motivation of the client, his or her willingness to change, and their access to services. A strong recovery plan, in my opinion, will consist of the following elements:

1. Individual counseling for the addict - weekly

2. Individual counseling for the spouse – at least every other week

3. Couple counseling – at least every other week

4. 12-step support group (SA, SAA, SLAA) for the addict – at least once per week (minimum of 3-5 times a week in early recovery)

5. Therapeutic process group for the addict – weekly

6. 12-step group for the spouse (COSA) – at least every other week (also available online)

Exercise

Questions for Consideration: Answer each question to the best of your ability, being as thorough as possible in your response.

1. Considering the affair or infidelity that has occurred in your marital relationship, what compulsive or addictive factors are present (if any)? How will you determine if you are dealing with an addiction or not?

2. How does the idea of this being an addiction impact your thoughts and feelings about the situation, the relationship, your spouse, and recovery from infidelity in general?

3. Taking into consideration those things that were discussed in this chapter, what have you found most helpful and why? How might having an understanding of sexual addiction help you in your relationship today?

Part II

PHASES OF INFIDELITY RECOVERY

CHAPTER FIVE

Phase One - Discovery

How Infidelity Is Discovered

Perhaps the most emotionally charged time in an infidelity situation is the point at which its existence is discovered. This is the point that the rubber meets the road in the relationship and things can get rather ugly quickly. Perhaps the most interesting discovery story told to me by a client was a young 26 year-old woman who said that she actually caught her husband in the act of having intercourse with another woman. He had gone out earlier that evening and was supposedly out with a couple of friends. After a few hours, she tried calling him to see what time he would be home. When she called, he had somehow unintentionally answered the phone and his wife could hear what sounded like two people having sex. One of the voices was distinctly female and the other male. Realizing that it was her husband, she drove to a local bar that he regularly frequented and saw his truck in the parking lot. She parked her car and upon walking up to the window of the truck, noticed her husband and another woman having sex. She confronted her husband, at which time the other woman went running across the parking lot with most of her clothes in her hands. Needless to say, this was a shocking discovery for the wife and unfortunately, the marriage did not last.

Although some individuals do discover an affair or infidelity by actually catching their spouse in the act of having sex with another person, that is not typical. In the high-technology world we live in today, it seems as though most affairs and infidelities are discovered through call history on cell phones, text messages, e-mail, and social media. Although I have not seen any conclusions from formal research, I would say that at least 75-85% of these events are discovered in this fashion. With electronic media, there is always a history, and in some cases, even a paper trail. I cannot count the number of people that have told me they found out that their wife or husband was cheating on them through such mediums. I would simply say that when phones and computers are used, discretion is difficult and it is just a matter of time before it is discovered. Does that deter or stop people? Absolutely not.

The Impact of Discovery

If you are reading this book, it is most likely because you have discovered that your spouse is cheating or your spouse caught you cheating. Either way, this is a horrific situation. When a person discovers that their spouse has been unfaithful, a multitude of emotions will flood the individual, overwhelming them to the point that they can potentially become numb or unresponsive. It can be so terrifying that the person may ultimately develop symptoms or characteristics of post traumatic stress disorder (PTSD).

Let's walk through a somewhat generic discovery of an affair or infidelity situation. Imagine for a moment that a man (we will call him Ed) has been involved in an eight-month long affair with a co-worker. The wife (Lisa) has had no suspicions of what was occurring up to this point. Ed had been working on the computer in the study one evening when he left to go play catch with their son. In his haste, he failed to properly log out of his account and subsequently, off of the computer. Lisa had gone in the room to put something away and noticed that the computer was still on and that an e-mail was visible on the screen. She began reading the e-mail, quickly becoming noticeably anxious and upset. She had stumbled across an e-mail from her husband to a woman he worked with. It spoke of feelings he had for this woman, how much he missed her, and how wonderful their recent business trip together and associated love-making had been. It also spoke of his dissatisfaction with his marriage and how much he looked forward to seeing her and how he wished they could be together more often.

As Lisa finished reading this e-mail, tears of immense sadness flowed down her cheeks. She could not believe what she had just read – the betrayal she felt and the deceit she had just uncovered. She was experiencing enormous emotional pain, but wanted desperately to know more. She decided while the opportunity presented itself, to look through the rest of Ed's e-mails. As she sifted through the numerous e-mails still in the system, she discovered countless others that her husband and his mistress had sent to each other. Some of these e-mails were sent weeks and even months earlier. It was at this point that Lisa realized this affair had been going on for quite some time. She was literally in shock, completely overwhelmed by what she had discovered. Lisa sat in the desk chair, numb and bewildered, staring aimlessly at the computer screen, wondering what she should do next. "Should I confront him?" "Should I leave him?" Should I kick him out?" "Are we looking at divorce?" she wondered.

After a few minutes of sitting in what felt like a trance, sounds of her husband and son coming into the house startled her back into conscious awareness. She wiped the tears from her eyes and face as she decided to pretend that nothing was wrong – at least until she figured out what to do next. Lisa knew this wouldn't be easy, but she felt very lost and confused at the present moment. She knew she needed a plan, but had no idea what that plan should look like.

Initial Feelings

It is apparent from this short depiction of the discovery of an infidelity that it can be a very difficult and challenging time. I have had women tell me that it not only changed the way they viewed their husband, it changed the way they viewed the marriage and even life as a whole. Many have stated that it made them question the validity of their marriage vows and whether the entire marriage had been one big lie. As demonstrated by this story, the variance and flood of emotions is extreme. Like Lisa, men and women in this situation are likely to experience sadness, disbelief, anger, jealousy, anxiety, confusion, numbness, resentment, frustration, sorrow, grief, and perhaps even guilt and self-loathing. There are no right or wrong emotions, and just about anything is possible. This short list is by no means meant to be all inclusive.

In addition to these various emotions, what really seems to stand out for men and women that discover their spouse is having an affair is the complete sense of betrayal they feel which subsequently leads them to question their entire marital relationship. They feel as though the whole thing has been built upon a lie, that everything they have worked for is destroyed, and that perhaps the whole relationship is just one big illusion – a nightmare if you will. It will eventually also cause them to question whether they can ever trust again, and whether relationships in general and marriage specifically are worth the risk.

Questions and Decision Points

Let's go back to the story of Lisa for a moment. She has discovered a horrible secret that her husband, Ed, has been keeping from her for quite a while. She is devastated and confused as we just discussed. She now has a very big decision to make – Who to tell or talk to about this. She is likely feeling very alone. She wants and needs to reach out to someone for support, encouragement, and advice. This is a tricky and delicate situation. She probably feels embarrassed and even guilty, falling into the trap of believing that she is somehow partly responsible for what her husband did. She may mistakenly believe that there must be something wrong with her for this to have occurred. Worse yet, she is likely to believe that this is what others will think and that she, her husband, and her family will be judged negatively for it.

Take a minute and think about who you might tell if you are or were someday in this situation. Parents might be a good choice. They are oftentimes a great source of support and wisdom. They love you and want the very best for you. That however, may not be such a wise decision.

The problem with telling your parents is that if you and your spouse recover and ultimately heal the relationship, his or her relationship with your parents may be forever tarnished. It also forces the parents to take sides. What about a sister or brother? Again, a great source of support, but the relationship between them and your spouse could be severely impacted. Friends are a good choice – especially if they are not too close to your spouse. I would caution you however, to make sure it is someone of the same gender or you may find yourself in a bad position should he or she decide to prey upon your vulnerability and pain. Another dynamic to be cautious about is telling a friend who has a spouse that is friends with your spouse. They will talk and the other couple will feel caught in the middle of all the drama. This can result in displaced loyalties as well as lost friendships. Regardless of who you decide to tell, make sure it is someone that will maintain confidences. It needs to be someone you trust will not share the information or gossip to others.

In addition to family and friends, you may want to consider professional contacts as well. For example, you will definitely want to seek counseling. I can't recommend this strongly enough. Counseling will be critical to your ability to make sense of what has happened, to rediscover who you are in the midst of this pain, and to make important decisions about your future. To find a good therapist, I would recommend going to the website of the American Association for Marriage and Family Therapy (www.aamft. org) and search their therapist locator service. You may also want to consider therapists you have heard others recommend in the past. I would find someone you feel comfortable talking to and who has a good knowledge of and experience with infidelity. Therapists typically charge by the hour. The actual fee varies by area, but on average it will be in the neighborhood of $85-150 per hour. Your insurance may pay this fee, partially or in full.

Another great source of professional support is clergy. If you have your own priest, pastor, rabbi etc. that is even better. Clergy are not necessarily trained counselors and you should not go to them for clinical counseling or in place of a therapist. They deal a lot with infidelity however, and are viewed as experts in the area of forgiveness and grief / loss. Spiritual healing is an important part of the process and in my opinion can make a definitive difference between success and failure in the overall recovery process. I have counseled many people who have been referred to me as a result of infidelity, particularly when the behavior is compulsive or an addiction is potentially present. When I see clients who have experienced infidelity, I always inquire about their level of spirituality and encourage them to consider spiritual or pastoral care as an adjunct to what I am doing. This has worked extremely well in the past and I recommend that you consider it as part of your recovery plan.

One other person that you will most definitely want to tell is your physician. This is important for the primary purpose of getting tested for the presence of a sexually transmitted disease. This process of doing so will significantly heighten your feelings of shame and embarrassment, but is absolutely necessary in order to adequately protect yourself. You don't even necessarily have to tell your story to get the tests done, but you may find the additional support helpful. I would recommend that you take a friend or other source of support with you if at all possible.

Holding It Together

In Lisa's case, she has not yet confronted her husband about the affair, but she has discovered it and has plenty of proof to confirm it. She is in a holding pattern of sorts while she decides what to do next. This is a very difficult place to be as she is being bombarded with various emotions, while at the same time, having to pretend that everything is fine. For example, she has to live and exist in close proximity to her husband. What if he wants to touch her? What does she tell the children? What does she do if she starts feeling overwhelmed and out of control? What does she do about her responsibilities at home, at work, and in the community? There is no perfect answer to these questions. Much is going to depend on the person, their coping skills, and level of resiliency. It is crucial that she still takes care of herself. It is important to get rest, eat a proper diet, and get plenty of exercise. This will be extremely difficult at times, but is absolutely necessary. She will also need to have time to herself to think, but must resist the temptation to withdrawal or isolate from family and friends. It is critical that she not stay in this transitional place long-term. She will need to decide who she trusts enough to talk to and make preparations to confront her spouse.

Things to Avoid

Knowing that an affair or infidelity has occurred is an extremely difficult and painful situation to have to deal with. It is worth mentioning that there are several things you want to avoid doing at this point in the recovery process. As you begin to make decisions and prepare to confront your spouse, you must, above all else, take care of yourself. You are no good to anyone in a dysfunctional state.

As stated earlier, you must eat, sleep and exercise. This is at the core of self-care. Next, avoid excessive drinking, illegal drugs, or use of heavy medications. These will alter your state of mind and cause you to think or do irrational things. Do not attack the other woman (man) verbally or physically. Doing so will not only jeopardize any leverage you have, but could get you thrown in jail as well. This would cost you financially, and could even result in legal problems down the road should you decide to divorce. It could also impact your job or career, not to mention your ability to visit with or have custody of your children.

I mentioned earlier in this discussion that you must avoid the temptation to withdrawal or isolate yourself from others. This simply isn't healthy and can cause problems in other areas of your life and in other relationships. You need to be around people much of the time. Balance that however, with your need to be alone. In contrast to wanting to be alone, do not use your spouse's affair as a reason to get even by having one of your own. That is just a dangerous and immature response. It would be very easy for someone to take advantage of your pain or for you to go looking for someone to take away some of that pain yourself through sex. The problem is that it won't work. The pain will still be there the next morning and you will likely feel enormous guilt and shame for sinking to the same level as your spouse. Be the better person and do what is right. Begin the process of healing and finding hope in the midst of chaos.

Exercise

Questions for Consideration: Answer each question to the best of your ability, being as thorough as possible in your response.

1. Describe who you would include in your circle of trust (and why) if you were to discover that your spouse was having an affair. Who would you intentionally not tell and why?

2. During the recovery process, what would you specifically do to take care of yourself? How would you know if these things were working?

3. Taking into consideration those things that were discussed in this chapter, what have you found most helpful and why? How might having an understanding of the discovery phase of the infidelity recovery model help you in your relationship today?

CHAPTER SIX

Phase Two – Confrontation

The second phase in the overall infidelity treatment process is that of confronting the person that had the affair or that was unfaithful. Although the word, confrontation, sounds harsh, it may be helpful to think of it as more of a meeting to simply acknowledge what has happened and to let your spouse know that the infidelity is exposed. This is an extremely complicated and challenging step however. It contains significant risk and a lot can go wrong. I will attempt to offer some suggestions and advice in the hope that this will be made easier and more successful. I will begin by simply saying that preparation and proper planning are critically important.

Preparation

At this point in the overall process, you have discovered the affair or infidelity and you have hopefully talked to someone about it – family, friend, therapist, and/or clergy. If not, that is fine, but most people find some initial comfort in being able to reach out to someone. It is not easy however. This person must be someone you trust and doing so still involves great vulnerability, as well as a significant amount of shame and embarrassment. You may want to consider having this person nearby or in a position where they can be reached during or following the confrontation with your spouse - the person that had the affair or infidelity.

The confrontation should take place relatively soon following the discovery. This is to preclude the individual from learning that their secret has been exposed or the escalation of a disagreement into a fight or physical altercation. There is no absolute ideal amount of time, but I would generally say that it should be done within 48-72 hours. This will give you time to cool off, reflect on where you are in life and in the marriage, and collect your thoughts about what you would like to say and perhaps the best way to make your points.

The confrontation should be planned in advance by simply telling your spouse you need to talk to him or her about some important matters. Block off time at a location that is physically safe and free of distractions. It should not be a public place and if you have kids, they should not be in the same location. Turn off all phones, computers, and other electronic devices that could prove to be disruptive. Set the time so that you both are alert and able to comprehend what is being said and discussed. Therefore, avoid late nights, early mornings, or immediately following work. Also allow yourselves enough time. You should not schedule it just before an activity, meeting, or special engagement. I would recommend having 3-4 hours available just in case. You also want to make sure you are not hungry or overly full when this meeting is conducted. Having some water available would be nice as well. Tissues or other care products should be on hand as appropriate. Finally, make sure you bring all applicable proof or documentation of the infidelity with you. Some people ask whether it is wise to have a third party there for moral support. I personally think that could be distracting. It may also cause the spouse to become extremely defensive and subsequently, shutdown. That being said however, I do feel that you should have someone you can call that you know would be available by phone. Related to this is the fact that you should have a place to go should you decide to leave for the night, a week, or even longer.

The Actual Confrontation

It is important to recognize that when you confront your spouse about the affair or infidelity, a lot of different things can happen. You can't necessarily predict exactly how he or she will respond, but you can make some tentative plans based on a few assumptions. You should first assume that he or she will likely deny everything at first. This is almost always the case and is the reason for you having your "proof" on hand. Be sure to make copies however as they may try to destroy these. I would recommend trying to make the initial conversation as straightforward and unemotional as possible. The objective here should be to let them know what you have discovered and that you have absolute proof of it. You are simply making sure they understand that things are in the open and that "the gig is up."

Another possible response from your spouse will be admitting to everything immediately. Faced with the truth literally staring them in the face, they may not see any point in trying to hide it any longer or cover it up. They may even be relieved that they have been caught, especially if they truly have feelings for this other person. In cases such as this, they may have simply been too scared to come forward and disclose the affair before it got to this point. Individuals such as these are oftentimes labeled "emotional cowards."

Another possible response will be to get angry and defensive, perhaps even trying to turn everything back on you. I remember talking to a spouse who had confronted her husband about an affair she discovered while looking at text messages on his phone. He immediately became enraged and started yelling at her for looking at his phone; accusing her of invading his privacy, and asking how she could do such a thing. Notice how the attention was diverted away from the affair and worse yet, became more about her looking at the phone than about his affair. If this happens, you must try to bring it back to the affair. You can take responsibility for your actions, but don't let the focus stay there. A possible response might be, "yes, perhaps it was inconsiderate of me to look at your phone, but we need to address what I found."

Once the initial discovery information is out on the table, it is important for you to sit down as a couple and decide what this means for your relationship. This may also be the point at which you discuss whether one of you should move out, at least temporarily. I have mixed views on this. First, I sincerely believe that it is difficult to work on a relationship if you are not living together. On the other hand however, I also believe that a short separation can give both partners time to think and reflect, while also enabling them to experience not having each other around and perhaps becoming more aware of what they both stand to lose.

I have had couples do both of these things with good results. More often than not however, the short separation seems to have better outcomes associated with it. If you have kids, your spouse will likely experience grief, loss, and loneliness associated with not seeing his or her children like they were used to prior to this point. That can also help in making the case for what is at stake. As stated before, you should make sure you have a place to go just in case, but since your spouse is the one who was unfaithful, they should be the one to leave if that is the decision that is made. You may be concerned that if your spouse leaves, he or she will simply go back to his or her lover. You can't control that and you must try not to obsess about that possibility.

If the affair is a deeply emotional one, asking your spouse whether they love the other person and whether they want to be with them or get a divorce is probably not a good question. You have already caught them off-guard and they need time to figure things out as well. I would recommend simply telling them that they need to decide who they want to be with (assuming you haven't already decided to permanently end the marriage) and give them a reasonable amount of time to decide (3-5 days should be sufficient). I would suggest telling them that they have that amount of time to decide, but should they decide to work on the marriage you expect just that – 100% effort towards saving the marriage. You also need to tell them that you expect them to eliminate all contact with the other individual or stop whatever acting out behaviors are involved (e.g., pornography, strip clubs, masturbation etc.). You must also outline what you expect with regards to counseling. These should be non-negotiable. For example, I would say something like, "You need to decide which one of us you would rather be with. You have until Wednesday at 5:00 p.m. to give me your decision. Should you decide to stay in the marriage, you will cut off all contact with (name of other person of known) forever, and attend counseling every week – both individually and with me as a couple. These things are non-negotiable and there are no guarantees that if you do these things that it will work, but I will give you and us the chance."

It is important that both of you realize that although many couples recover from infidelity, it isn't easy and it can be an extremely long and painful process. There are no guarantees. You may work hard and do everything right only to discover that you just can't seem to make it work. At least then you will know and you won't be wondering in the future if things could have been different; if the marriage could have been saved had you only tried. If you do decide to work on the marriage, boundaries such as who will sleep where must be negotiated. There are no perfect answers on many of these issues. Each couple is different and unique. I think it would be difficult for the two of you to sleep in the same bed at first and I would recommend that you sleep in different rooms with the goal being to eventually return to the same bed and a life of passion and love at some point in the future. Many of the couples I have worked with have done just that and it is a beautiful and heartwarming process to witness and be a part of.

I would not make the confrontation meeting a time to discuss everything that is wrong in the marriage and why the affair or infidelity occurred in the first place. The goal is to get things out on the table and start making a decision as to what comes next. The healing process should be slow and methodical. If your spouse decides to stay and work on the marriage then you should make a counseling appointment for the two of you as a couple as soon as possible. You may already want to have one made just in case and then cancel it if he or she decides they don't want to stay. Another option is to give them the responsibility for making the appointment. You will get a feel for their commitment level by whether or not they actually follow through and make the appointment. They also can't blame you then for making the appointment at a bad time or going to a therapist they are unhappy with. You will want to call your support person and let them know how things went. They can then either stand-down and relax, knowing that you are alright; or engage on a deeper level depending on your personal needs.

It is important that the conversation remains civil and that you try to avoid name-calling. You will also obtain much better results if you attempt to treat each other with dignity and respect. Regardless of the behavior, you should keep in mind that you are still husband and wife and that you got married in the first place out of love for one another. If the discussion escalates, you need to leave and call the police if necessary. Engage your support person and get whatever assistance you need to remain physically safe. I personally do not think it should ever get to that point, but it does happen and you need to be cautious.

Other Post-Meeting Considerations

Another important consideration in these situations is what you are going to tell the children. I would not advise trying to keep this all a secret, but the conversation should be age-appropriate and you should not seek to damage the children's relationship with your spouse, regardless of what decisions are reached. I would not necessarily tell them that an affair occurred or that their mother or father cheated. They don't need to know this. It is about respect and preserving relationships. Depending on the age, you may want to simply say that you and your wife / husband are having some relationship problems and that you are going to work hard to make things better again (assuming that is the decision that has been reached). If not, I would just say that you and your wife / husband are having really big problems in the relationship and when appropriate to do so, follow it up with a discussion regarding the decision not to stay married. You will want to reassure them that it is not about them, anything they did or didn't do, and that you both love them with all of your hearts. I would also recommend counseling for the children and perhaps even for the whole family so that various resultant emotions and thoughts can be stated and processed as appropriate.

I remember as a child, being asked by my parents who I would rather live with – my mother or my father. I told them I could not make such a decision. I also knew that I would want to stay with my brother. In the end, my parents did not divorce, but to this day, I do not know if they were happy together. They are both deceased now so I guess I will never know for sure.

Divorce has a major impact on all members of the family, regardless of age. Research also shows however, that more harm can occur when parents stay together just for the kids. The bottom line – don't stay in the marriage simply to avoid hurting the children. It will likely do more harm than a divorce itself would. A good therapist can be a significant source of help for the children regardless of whether you decide to stay together or not.

Exercise

Questions for Consideration: Answer each question to the best of your ability, being as thorough as possible in your response.

1. Describe how you will or would make the decision as to remaining in the marriage following an infidelity. What are the major factors for consideration?

2. If a confrontation meeting has not yet occurred, describe the steps you need to take to ensure that it is conducted appropriately and that your intended goals of the meeting are reached?

3. What considerations are important in making the determination to initially separate? Where would you go and how would you take care of yourself financially? What would you tell your children?

4. Taking into consideration those things that were discussed in this chapter, what have you found most helpful and why? How might having an understanding of the confrontation phase of recovery from infidelity help you in your relationship today?

CHAPTER SEVEN

Phase Three – Decision

The next phase is really more of a decision point, but is a critical one nonetheless. The third phase of the infidelity recovery process involves making the decision to either stay and work on the marriage or separate and possibly even divorce. I often tell couples considering divorce that by committing to and engaging in the recovery process, they will be able to either repair their marriage or will, as a minimum, know that they at least tried. I attempt to help couples understand how devastating it would be for them to find themselves a year or even five years down the road, wondering if they could have possibly saved their marriage had they only put forth more effort. This is an emotionally charged decision however, and one that should not be made lightly. Couples that find themselves in this unfortunate position should try to think through this situation thoroughly. An individual facing this decision should seek advice and Divine guidance as appropriate. It should not be a decision that is made on the fly, without much focused thought, and considerable prayer. The decision should be based on logic, accounting for all potential consequences and effects – both direct and indirect. It is also worth noting that this decision should ideally involve both partners. Although they may not agree on the course of action, both are impacted by the outcome.

Betraying Partner

Most of the book thus far has been focused on the spouse of the person who had the affair or that was unfaithful (the injured partner). It is now time to direct attention to the person who had the affair (the betraying partner). Like the spouse, this person needs to make a decision as to whether or not he or she is going to stay in the marriage as well. The emotions may be different and the decision making process may take a slightly different course, but both individuals have an enormously difficult decision to make. For the purpose of discussion, I will typically refer to the spouse of the individual that had the affair or infidelity as the "injured partner." Likewise, I will refer to the person that had the affair or infidelity as the "betraying partner." These terms are being used in order to promote common terminology, while also making an attempt to minimize additional feelings of shame.

In having an affair or being unfaithful to your spouse, you crossed a line that has impacted the two of you and the rest of your family greatly. You may not have known that line existed when you betrayed your spouse, but ignorance is not a defense and does not mean that the behavior is acceptable or that it is in any way condoned. Perhaps you should have had a conversation with your spouse in which the parameters of acceptable behavior were discussed, but you didn't or if you did, you did not do a very good job of listening to your spouse and taking into consideration his or her feelings and wishes on the matter. It is not something that can be redone or taken back.

You now need to take a hard look at your marriage and the behaviors you are or have been engaged in. As you recall from earlier chapters, affairs happen for many different reasons. Some of these are intrapersonal (individual) and others are interpersonal (relational). Regardless of the reasons, your marriage can be saved if you and your spouse want it to be and are willing to put forth the required effort. This chapter is devoted to the first part – determining if you actually want to or not. Subsequent chapters will then show you how.

Regardless how long you have been married, you most likely got married because you fell in love with each other. You may have also gotten married because of a pregnancy, you thought your financial situation would be better living together with two incomes, you or your spouse were going into the military or off to college, you were tired of being alone, you didn't think you could find anyone else, you wanted to leave the small town you grew up in, and perhaps a host of other reasons. My personal belief is that although several of these reasons may apply in your situation, you still got married because you fell in love. You may deny this, but I have a hard time believing that people marry each other if they don't love one another – or at least think they do.

Assuming that you at one point loved your spouse, I feel that it is reasonable to assume that you can again. It may even be safe to assume that you still do. One of the potential challenges of the recovery process will be falling in love with each other again. Before we get to that point however, we have to still decide whether you actually want to make this relationship work. Many times when a person gets involved with another individual outside of the marriage, they start to think that he or she would make a much better partner or spouse. Thus, the grass once again becomes greener on the other side of the fence. This is a dangerous place to be since it involves fantasy. In other words, it is not anchored in reality. You will focus on the strengths of the other person while simultaneously focusing on the weaknesses of your spouse. This is a no-win situation and will ultimately lead to problems. In this situation it is only a matter of time before you "jump ship" to be with the other person or do everything in your power to drive your spouse to the point that he or she leaves you or kicks you out. This passive-aggressive behavior lessens your guilt because you can say, "I didn't leave her; she left me or kicked me out. It was her choice."

You need to step back from the excitement and passion of your relationship with this other individual and honestly look at what you love about your spouse. Make a list of the qualities that you most admire and appreciate in your spouse. What does he or she do for you that you appreciate? What does he or she do with you that you enjoy? What did you like most about him or her when you first got married? What was the first thing you noticed about him or her when you met? Now imagine not having that person to do these things for you or with you. What does that look like? In the early stages of a relationship, we have blinders on that cause us to only notice the good qualities or the things we like and admire about that individual. As the relationship matures however, the blinders come off and we start to notice all the bad things as well. Therefore, in a more mature marriage, we will start to notice, and subsequently focus on the negative things in our spouse while noticing positive things in people we may have recently met or gotten involved in a relationship with.

When two people meet, they "fall" for each other and develop what is referred to as romantic love. This love is fun, exciting, spontaneous, and passionate. As couples mature in their relationship, they develop companionate love. This love is more secure, stable, logical, and enduring. We sometimes fail to see the wonderful qualities in this latter category of love because it doesn't feel as exciting and fun. This is particularly true when we develop feelings for another person – feelings that can be qualified as fun, exciting, passionate, and spontaneous. We need to bring these qualities back into our marriage, while also recognizing the wonderful characteristics of the companionate love that already exist. Things that are often new seem better just because they are new. We need to resist this, while also searching for ways to keep our marriage exciting and passionate.

In order to be able to accurately and honestly assess your marital situation, it is critical that you stop seeing the other person until such time that you have made a decision as to whether you are going to work on repairing your marriage. I have had many husbands and wives tell me in describing their spouse who had the affair that it is like he or she is trying to have the best of both worlds. A decision needs to be made. It is only fair to you, your spouse, and to the other person. The critical element is that the decision to stay or leave must be made carefully. There is a lot riding on it.

I am sure that by now you are asking yourself how such an important decision is made. There is no mathematical equation or statistical formula to give you a final answer. Unlike a popular television show a few years back, you do not have any lifelines available to you. What you do have however, is a sound mind; a spouse; good friends; loving family; and an all-knowing, all-powerful eternal God that can each help you in their own special and unique way. In other words, you are not alone. Seek help when necessary, particularly from those that know you best. Think about your spouse and your marriage and what things were like when you were dating and were first married. How would you feel about your marriage right now if things were still that way? Think about how you met and what most attracted you to him or her. Do those things still exist or still attract you? If your spouse has changed physically, has that become an obstacle or barrier? In what ways is she even more beautiful? In what ways is he even more handsome?

Now think about the goals and dreams you have set for yourself as a couple. Have you dreamed of growing old together? Have you dreamed of raising the children and having the house to yourself as you look forward to spoiling the grandchildren? Have you dreamed of retirement and being able to travel or invest energy in hobbies and interests? What will come of these things if you decide not to stay? Now think of the affair partner. Look past the romantic love - does this person really make you feel as comfortable and secure as your spouse? It may be difficult to do, but imagine yourself 10-25 years from now - with both your spouse and with the other person. How does that feel? Can you honestly say that the image of being with this other person is better?

I recognize that you and your spouse are having problems in your marriage. If that wasn't the case, you would not be reading this book. I know that you and your spouse are both suffering significant pain. I just ask that you completely weigh your options and consider all the facts prior to making such an important, potentially life-altering decision. I cannot think of very many reasons why a person would not want to at least try to repair the marriage. I would think that the thought of not knowing whether I could have potentially saved my marriage would be almost too difficult to handle. A baseball player will never know whether he will hit a homerun unless he steps up to the plate and takes a swing. You need to step up to the plate and take a swing. As I stated earlier, you won't know unless you try.

Up to this point, the discussion of whether to stay in the marriage has been limited to situations in which there is an affair partner. Keep in mind that this affair partner can be someone that is physically present - as in an affair with a colleague at work, or it can be a person you have met online (e.g., via chat, e-mail, social media, or dating sites, but have not yet met in person). The dynamics are similar – the perceived availability of another person which subsequently implies a choice between two potential partners (the spouse and the affair partner). The infidelity can however, take other forms as previously discussed (e.g., pornography, masturbation, and strip clubs etc.). In these cases there may not be a perceived choice between two different people. It may be a choice of whether to stay with the spouse or to leave. Some may equate this choice to leave with freedom to act out and do whatever they want sexually without there being anyone there to care or complain. This perceived freedom will likely be short lived and will eventually give way to loneliness. I do not know very many people, if any, who truly enjoy being single and want to remain that way forever. I doubt you do either. It may look appealing now, but it won't last.

Injured Partner

Although both partners have to make a decision as to whether to stay in the marriage or not, the dynamics behind these decisions are quite different. The betraying partner or person having the affair has to ultimately decide whether he or she would rather be with their spouse or with the affair partner. In most cases, this simply comes down to choosing between two alternatives. I don't say that to minimize the importance or magnitude of the situation. This is serious and I in no way mean to trivialize it.

The injured partner however, has to account for feelings of betrayal and emotional pain that may be too great to overcome. They have to decide whether they want to and can forgive their spouse for what has taken place. They also need to decide if they want to expend the energy necessary to repair the marriage – even if there are no guarantees that these efforts will be successful. It may take years to work through the issues surrounding the affair and to rebuild the relationship. It will be a challenging and extremely difficult process that will require among other things, a lot of persistence.

When you discover the affair or infidelity, the trust you have in your spouse will go away – until it resembles a gas gage sitting on empty. Rebuilding this trust is perhaps the most difficult and longest part of the recovery process. When couples initially get together, the trust level is usually quite high; a possible exception being a situation where one or both individuals have been hurt by others in the past. When an infidelity occurs, you no longer trust your spouse so he or she has to earn that trust back. This will take a considerable amount of time and effort.

The fear is that this trust will possibly never be restored. This is a real possibility and is a critical part of your decision to stay in the marriage or not. The actual process and mechanics of rebuilding this trust will be discussed in subsequent chapters.

When you discover the affair or infidelity and the subsequent trust in your spouse goes away, you need to begin asking yourself whether you honestly think you can ever completely trust him or her again. When answering this question, try to consider all facets of your relationship, past experiences in which you have been hurt (by both your spouse and by others), aspects of your personality that may make it more or less likely to trust again, and what he or she would likely have to do to earn your trust again. This is going to be a tough road and you need to assess whether you have the right equipment and are prepared for the journey. The ultimate question you will need to answer is "If we both give it our best effort, will I likely be able to trust him (her) again and am I willing to put forth this kind of effort considering the fact that there are no guarantees?"

Tied to the question of trust and effort is the concept of forgiveness. You need to ask yourself whether you can forgive your spouse for the pain he or she has caused you. Forgiveness does not and never will equal forgetting. Instead, it has more to do with recognizing that you have been hurt by another person and are willing to let go of the pain and any subsequent ill feelings towards that individual. When we resist forgiving a person, we expend an incredible amount of energy in holding on to feelings of anger, resentment, and bitterness. Forgiveness doesn't mean you approve of or even condone the behavior. It also doesn't mean you are going to give the person another chance or that you are going to stay in the relationship. I believe it has more to do with making a conscious choice to be free, no longer being held captive by the actions of another person. It means you value yourself enough to move forward with or without the other person. It is about taking the power for your own happiness and life satisfaction away from the other person and giving it back to yourself. In other words, forgiveness equates to making ourselves responsible for our own destiny and happiness, regardless of what others do or don't do. It then becomes an issue of personal empowerment.

The decision of whether to stay in the marriage is compounded significantly by past events. In other words, it will be easier to decide to stay if this is the first time an affair or infidelity has occurred. When similar events have happened before this it becomes "more of the same." You will begin to doubt whether he or she is actually capable of changing or whether he or she wants to in the first place. You will begin asking yourself questions such as "why bother? He or she is only going to do it again. It is just a matter of time." Do these statements and/or questions sound familiar? It may also be compounded by the betrayal of other significant people in your life. For example, if you have been hurt in previous relationships, your ability to trust your spouse and others may be greatly diminished. Similarly, if key people such as parents, boyfriends or girlfriends, spouses, and other friends have not been there for you when you needed them most, you will likely have a much harder time learning to trust others and will subsequently, have a harder time learning to trust your spouse again – or even wanting to try.

While serving as a Chaplain in a Marine unit, I had a spouse tell me that her husband was *going* to beat her. Notice the future tense of this statement. I asked her if he was currently beating her. She said no, but that he would. I asked her how she knew this and she stated "because all of my previous boyfriends have." She was telling me that she expected to be beat because that is simply what others did to her. She figured it was just a matter of time. Similarly, if you have been cheated on before, you may think that all men cheat or that is simply the way life is and that you need to learn to adapt to the situation. This is not true. You deserve better and you have to separate this person and this situation from others in your life. The decision of whether to stay is grounded heavily in the issues of trust and, forgiveness.

A final aspect of this decision rests heavily upon your feelings towards him or her. In other words, when separating the affair or infidelity away from the situation momentarily, what do you honestly feel? Do you love this person? Do you want to have a life together? Are things generally good in the relationship? This last question is somewhat loaded and must be applied cautiously because there is a good chance that problems in the marriage have been significant contributors to the affair or infidelity. If things were good, it stands to reason that the affair or infidelity would not have occurred. That does not mean however, that things can't be good again. I have had couples say things such as "when the relationship is good, things are really good; but when the relationship is bad, it is really bad." This tells me that there are strengths in the relationship, that there are things the couple has to work through; but that if they can do that, they can have a great marriage. Similarly, examine the really good moments in your relationship. What are those like for you? If that is what you experienced on a daily basis, would you want to stay in the marriage?

Exercise

Questions for Consideration: Answer each question to the best of your ability, being as thorough as possible in your response.

1. Discuss your intentions pertaining to remaining in the marriage. What factors are important to this decision? Discuss the pros and cons of each choice.

2. Discuss your thoughts about trusting your spouse again. Do you think you can (why or why not)? What will it take on your part and on theirs to make this happen?

3. When considering the topic of forgiveness, how important do you feel this is? Is forgiveness possible in your relationship (why or why not)? What will need to happen for forgiveness to occur?

4. Taking into consideration those things that were discussed in this chapter, what have you found most helpful and why? How might having an understanding of the decision phase of recovery from infidelity help you in your relationship today?

CHAPTER EIGHT

Phase Four — Disclosure

One of the most challenging aspects of recovery from infidelity and sexual addiction is disclosure. You may be asking yourself what disclosure is and what the process actually entails. Simply stated, disclosure has to do with "coming clean" about everything that has taken place. In some cases, there is no real need for additional disclosure following the confrontation phase of recovery because the spouse already knows everything, having discovered it on his or her own. In other cases however, the spouse only knows a portion of what has taken place. In cases such as this, the spouse only has a piece of the puzzle, but unfortunately, will likely be completely unaware of this fact. When a discovery is made, the spouse will not know if they know everything or not. They may assume that there is more regardless of whether or not that is true, or they may mistakenly believe that they know everything that has occurred – another faulty assumption at best.

I have had several individuals, both men and women, ask me if they should disclose an affair that happened years prior which their spouse knows nothing about. My response is generally consistent with that of most researchers and relationship experts. Specifically, I tell them that if there is virtually no chance of the spouse discovering the affair and if the individual has done the work necessary to ensure that another affair of act of infidelity does not occur then they probably should not reveal something that has taken place so long ago. Don't misunderstand what I am saying. I am not an advocate of secret keeping. I do not feel that spouses should keep things from one another. They should be open and honest with one another to the fullest extent possible. In this particular case however, I do not feel that disclosure would serve any positive purpose other than relieving some burden of guilt in the case of the confessor. If that is the sole reason for the disclosure, then it should not take place. It is therefore incumbent upon the person considering such a disclosure to be perfectly honest in their assessment of the reasons for doing so.

In most cases of infidelity, an individual discovers that their partner has been having or has had an affair, a relationship, or perhaps they caught their husband or wife engaging in some form of inappropriate sexual behavior. What they discovered however, is not the whole truth – it is only a snapshot or a piece of the full picture. Let's look at a couple of examples. Sharon is a twenty-five year old wife who recently woke up in the middle of the night only to find her husband, Jeff, on the computer looking at nude pictures of barely legal females, videos of couples engaging in sexual intercourse, and one video of women acting out sexually with one another. When confronted by his shocked and confused wife, Jeff said that this was the first time he had ever done this. Sharon, wanting desperately to believe Jeff, knew better and trusted her instincts that this was not the first and only time. Although she had no proof, she was certain that Jeff was lying.

Samuel and Tina had been married almost twenty years when Samuel discovered some text messages and e-mails confirming an affair and sexual relationship between Tina and a man named Mark. From what Samuel could tell, the affair had been going on about four months. When he confronted Tina about the affair, she admitted to the relationship, but stated that it was the first time and that it had only been going on a few months as Samuel suspected. The reality however, was that this was the tenth affair Tina has had since she and Samuel got married. Additionally, Tina is addicted to sex, having slept with more than two hundred men and another hundred women during the past twenty years. Additionally, she has been a member of a very active swinger's club, having had more than fifty threesomes over the last five years. Samuel knows nothing about any of these other affairs. Tina has been very discreet up to this point and in effect, has successfully led two separate and distinct lives.

I have heard many say that the first time a person receives a speeding ticket is not the first time the individual ever sped. Although it would be unfair to draw the same conclusion with regards to affairs and infidelity, it is likely that this is not the first time he or she engaged in the behavior or at least considered it. It is also fair to consider that although this may or may not be the first time that the individual engaged in this specific behavior, it is fair to assume that there have probably been other types of behaviors that the individual has engaged in, currently or in the past. This is especially true when considering activities such as pornography, strip clubs, soliciting prostitutes or escorts, as well as various cyber activities such as erotic e-mail and chat.

In the case scenarios previously presented, I would say that Sharon is valid in her suspicions that this was not the first time Jeff had been viewing pornography. In fact, it is likely that he had been doing so for quite some time, possibly even throughout the duration of the couple's marriage – perhaps even longer. While this may not be the case, it is a definite possibility and the idea should not be rejected prematurely. In the second case, Samuel discovered that Tina had been having an affair, but she stated that it was the first time and that there had been no previous relationships. Lacking proof, Samuel has no real reason not to believe her, but the hidden truth is that Tina is a sex addict and had had numerous sexual relationships and affairs. As stated in the case scenario, she has been living a double life as both a sex addict and a devoted wife. The real question then ultimately becomes, "how does one know if there is more to the story – things that he or she has not yet revealed?"

Disclosure is a very important part of the recovery process. In fact, I would contend that recovery from a current or recent infidelity is not even possible without a full disclosure. The problem is that the spouse is already hurting so the additional information or knowledge may be too much for them and subsequently, the relationship to handle. Therefore, the injured partner or spouse must be prepared emotionally for the disclosure. This is best accomplished through individual counseling with the goal being that a full disclosure will ultimately occur at a future time when both partners and both individual therapists can actually be present. There may also be a desire or need for other individuals to be present in an effort to offer support and encouragement as applicable.

The person who had the affair or infidelity must also be prepared for the disclosure so that he or she can communicate all that occurred in a meaningful and emotionally relevant way. Most individuals do not make a full disclosure initially on their own because of shame and guilt, as well as the accompanying fear that by doing so the consequences will be worse. In the case of a relationship, their greatest fear is that a full disclosure will result in their partner or spouse leaving them. It is like the child who hits his sister and doesn't tell mom when asked about it out of fear that he will be punished. Fear is a major motivator for keeping secrets and it makes sense that you would be reluctant to tell your spouse everything if doing so might cause him or her to leave you. Be aware however, that things will be much worse if they discover the information on their own.

One of the difficulties of disclosure is making the decision of how much to disclose. There are some relationship professionals who believe that disclosure should occur at one time, confessing everything that has happened and sharing as many details as reasonably possible. This is commonly referred to as the shotgun approach. Another school of thought however, posits that disclosure should occur in steps with information being disclosed incrementally over time. I personally prefer the idea of a full disclosure at one point in time since repeated disclosures make it difficult to move on and each disclosure can serve as a means by which the individual can become re-traumatized. If there is an abundance of information to disclose however, it may be necessary to perform an incremental disclosure.

A second and related problem with disclosures is that of memory. Many of the men and women I have counseled who have engaged in multiple affairs or have participated in a variety of sexual behaviors have had tremendous difficulty remembering all of the pertinent details and information applicable to the infidelity. To the spouse or partner, this lack of detail or confusion of facts comes across as deceit and betrayal. In other words, the perception is that they don't remember because they don't want to or are unwilling to. This dynamic occurs more often than not.

Disclosure needs to be complete and therefore must be as accurate as possible. Getting details, even small ones, wrong will cause the spouse to question the entire disclosure and will likely result in him or her losing faith in the sincerity of both the disclosure and the recovery as a whole. The smallest error can jeopardize the entire process. Therefore, it must be done right. I prefer to have clients write down the disclosure – word for word - just as they intend to communicate it verbally. I then go through every detail with them, asking every possible question I can so that there is as little doubt as possible that the details laid out on paper happened just the way it says they did. I want the client to be absolutely sure of every known fact and communicate it accordingly. In cases where information is not completely known, it is best that the client be honest in stating that they don't know or that they don't remember. The worst thing they can do at this point is to make something up simply to fill in the blanks. Although the spouse will not appreciate the lack of detail or absence of facts, it will be much better than out-right lying.

In addition to factual content, the person making the disclosure must also communicate sincerity, empathy, and remorse. The disclosure should not be accomplished until this is possible. Therefore, some amount of individual counseling prior to the disclosure is essential. I will have the client practice communicating the disclosure so that the right emotions are communicated each and every time both verbally and nonverbally. The spouse wants to know details, but more importantly, they want to know that their partner understands what they are feeling and that they can actually feel or empathize with their pain or hurt. They also want the person to be remorseful and to communicate a desire and commitment to change and to know that something like this will never happen again. An important aspect of the disclosure is that all of these factors are critical to the success of the overall disclosure and will likely play a significant role in the decision to continue working on the relationship and associated recovery from infidelity.

The spouse that is receiving the disclosure must be emotionally present and in a state of mind that will allow him or her to simply listen to what is being said. They will have their therapist and possibly a supportive friend present to help them deal with feelings that arise through the disclosure process. The disclosure will not be easy for either partner. If they are both adequately prepared and honest in communicating what happened and their feelings surrounding it then the disclosure should facilitate healing. One warning worth mentioning however, is that the spouse to whom the disclosure is being made will probably want answers pertaining to why the affair or infidelity occurred. This may be an unrealistic expectation in the early stages of recovery however. The person making the disclosure may simply want to say something such as "I want to give you those answers. I just don't know the answers myself yet. That is in part why I am in counseling and I am confident that I will figure it out. As soon as I know, I will share that with you. I have been poor at keeping my promises to you up to this point, but this is one I fully intend to keep."

Exercise

Questions for Consideration: Answer each question to the best of your ability, being as thorough as possible in your response.

1. What aspects or elements of the disclosure process do you feel are still necessary for you to be able to have a successful disclosure with your partner or spouse?

2. Assuming the disclosure has not yet occurred, what do you anticipate as being the most difficult or challenging parts?

3. Describe your support system. How and in what ways will you utilize this support system in the disclosure process?

4. Taking into consideration those things that were discussed in this chapter, what have you found most helpful and why? How might having an understanding of the disclosure phase of recovery from infidelity help you in your relationship today?

CHAPTER NINE

Phase Five – Rebuilding

Once the difficult decision of whether to stay and work on the marriage has been made, the couple enters into the longest part of the recovery process, the rebuilding phase. It is worth noting that the couple may not be fully committed to the idea of staying together at this point, but are at least willing to keep an open mind and make an honest attempt to do so. There are many different considerations as a couple works on rebuilding their marriage following an infidelity and I will attempt to discuss each of them in this chapter.

Question of Separation

There are differing viewpoints on the issue of whether an initial separation is necessary or desirable. I believe that a short initial separation could be helpful as it will enable the couple to reflect on the situation and whether or not they want to work on the marriage. If the betraying partner is asked to leave then it also sends the message that the behavior is wrong and that it won't be tolerated. In other words, it helps to establish or solidify a boundary. Since the rebuilding phase technically begins following the decision to work on the marriage, separation should occur prior to this point if it is going to occur at all.

Some couples do however, decide to enter into a dating or courting type of relationship in which they live apart and simply begin dating again, as if they had just met and are trying to establish a relationship and get to know each other. In some cases, this works extremely well as it allows the couple to slow down and rebuild the relationship from the ground up in a structured and methodical manner. The downside is that by not living together, they may not have the ability to work on the significant relational issues that played a critical role in facilitating the affair or infidelity.

Seeking Help

Individual Counseling

This is the point at which the couple needs to form their support team. Perhaps the most important part of this will be entering into counseling and selecting the therapist(s) involved in that process. I would recommend that you begin by considering what you need as individuals and as a couple. You and your spouse have been affected in profound ways by the infidelity – individually and collectively. Therefore, it makes sense for you and your spouse to participate in both individual and couple counseling. This may sound like a lot of counseling, but the issues that you are dealing with on an individual level are different, although related to the issues you are dealing with as a couple. Therefore, you would each ideally have an hour of individual counseling per week, as well as an hour of couple counseling per week.

Individual counseling for the person that committed the infidelity or had the affair should focus on issues within the individual that contributed to the affair occurring. Some of the things that need addressing (not an all-inclusive list) include: family of origin issues (childhood stuff), attachment issues (parents or caretakers, siblings, friendships, and romantic relationships throughout the lifespan), stress management and coping skills, sexuality, intimacy, work-life balance, alcohol and drug abuse, addictions, pertinent medical issues, and life stressors.

When working with individuals who have been unfaithful, I want to know what purpose or need the behavior was filling in their life. For example, pornography may have become a way of coping with work stress; an affair partner may have been a means through which the person could obtain validation, affection, or intimacy that he or she felt they were not receiving at home. Affairs and infidelity, in my opinion, serve as a way to fill a void. In many cases however, the individual is not consciously aware of exactly what that void entails. This is the primary reason why I feel individual counseling is so important. As a therapist, I want to help the individual discover why the affair happened and what purpose it served. By knowing that, he or she can then start to fix the problem and repair the relationship.

You may be thinking that you have no idea where to start and what purpose the infidelity could possibly be serving. Don't get lulled into the trap of thinking that it is all about sex – it isn't. This is especially true when considering sexual addiction. If you think you may be dealing with an addiction, I encourage you to re-read chapter four. I have had people engage in inappropriate sexual behaviors out of boredom, anger, stress, and loneliness to name just a few examples. The point is that emotions can play a major role in triggering or contributing to infidelity. Even more significant, I have seen numerous individuals engage in various behaviors in response to a desire for a deeper level of intimacy or attachment within the relationship. Many researchers go as far as to refer to infidelity as an attachment or intimacy disorder. This is a very accurate statement in my opinion since most people that I have counseled regarding infidelity admit to feeling neglected or abandoned in their marital relationship. They feel as though they are not important to their spouse and as a result, feel unloved, unappreciated, and/or disrespected. I would contend that if you want to minimize or even prevent an affair from occurring, make sure you both feel loved, appreciated, and respected throughout the course of the relationship.

For the injured partner, individual counseling will take a slightly different direction. Although the issues regarding why the affair or infidelity took place still apply (particularly the relational issues), much of what the spouse is dealing with pertains to issues of self-worth. They are oftentimes wondering what was so wrong with them that their spouse had to seek sexual release and comfort through other men and/or women, on or offline. It is also important however, to examine the same family of origin, coping, attachment, intimacy, and sexual issues as the person who actually had the affair. The key point here is that infidelity does not occur in a vacuum. There are issues specific to each person individually, as well as issues relating to the marriage that need to be addressed. Long-term healing and recovery requires a thorough examination of all these issues. As previously stated, I would recommend individual counseling at an initial frequency of once per week dropping down to every other week and then to once per month. With time, the frequency will lower even further to a quarterly or possibly less frequent basis.

Group Counseling

Another counseling modality that can prove extremely valuable in cases of infidelity is group counseling. It may be difficult at first to entertain the notion of group counseling due to shame, embarrassment, and general privacy concerns, but group counseling is among the most effective interventions that a therapist can draw from. There is an enormous sense of strength and relief that comes from being among other people going through the same thing. They offer each other encouragement, hope, and practical advice. I have had countless individuals come to me, surprised at how helpful being in an environment that provided both support and accountability was to the overall rebuilding and recovery process. This is particularly significant in cases where addiction may be an issue.

Most individuals when they hear the recommendation from their therapist to attend a group immediately feel that they will be judged, criticized, and condemned. Even betrayed partners feel that they will be made to feel as less of a wife or husband because their spouse had an affair or engaged in some form of infidelity. The reasoning again being that it is somehow their fault. The good news is that the group has the opposite impact and will help the person realize that it isn't their fault and that they are not a bad person or less of a man or woman as a result of the infidelity. The groups that I have witnessed provide strength and encouragement to all who attend and lovingly confront any misguided thinking. Most therapists run groups or know of a therapist that does. These groups may not specifically be tailored towards infidelity however, and may instead, be called men's issues or women's issues. It is worth checking these groups out in an attempt to find one that fits your specific needs and desires. I would recommend a weekly group that you feel would be worth attending for possibly more than a year. I know of one therapist who has facilitated a men's issues group for almost nine years now – with some of the same men in attendance the entire time. Group therapy is also a very cost effective way of obtaining long-term therapy.

Couple Counseling

Couple counseling is a critical element, but may prove to be among the most demanding in the rebuilding process. It is important, like that of any counseling, to find the right therapist. Research repeatedly shows that effectiveness in therapy is not as much related to what the therapist does (methods) as it is to factors related to resiliency of the client and various aspects of the therapeutic relationship. You need to find a therapist that you feel is unbiased and that can relate to what you are both going through. Gender and age should not be important, but they might be. You should not feel as though the therapist and your spouse are ganging up on you. Ultimately, you should feel safe to open up to this person in the security of their office or other suitable counseling location.

Couple counseling should be a weekly endeavor and although the specific goals and objectives will vary from couple to couple, counseling should focus on issues within the marriage that are problematic, particularly those that may have contributed to the infidelity. The assumption I am making is that there have been relational problems existing in your marriage for months, and more likely, years. These relational problems are foundational to treating the couple and subsequently, recovering from the infidelity.

The therapist should address communication within the marriage, exploring questions such as how often the couple sits down and engages in meaningful conversation and what kinds of things they generally talk about. Too often, the topic of conversation turns to issues involving the children and managing the home. This is really sad because it enables couples to lose focus on themselves as a couple and all the wonderful things that they actually have to talk about and share with one another.

It is likely that you do not communicate very well with your spouse. It is awkward and you probably don't feel that you have the time or perhaps even the desire to do so. Even couples who do attempt to communicate are rarely able to do so free of distractions such as children, television, work, cell phones etc. It is vitally important that you and your spouse sit down together every day and engage in fulfilling conversation free of distractions.

Tied to the concept of communication and conversation is that of arguments and disagreements. All couples argue, but some do it much better than others. By this, I mean that some couples argue or disagree in a manner that is still respectful and with a clearly conceived and perhaps even articulated goal. For these couples, winning the argument is not the goal, building a better relationship is. They also understand the concept that sometimes people need to agree to disagree. It is important for the therapist to look at the kinds of issues that the couple typically argues about. This may offer significant insight into what the couple views as important and the manner in which they go about resolving conflict.

Other issues that the couple therapist will likely attempt to resolve or at least intentionally devote attention to include such things as: trust, forgiveness, individual and partner needs, intimacy, sexuality, roles and responsibilities, children and parenting, stress and coping, extended family relationships and friendships, and family financial stress. Although I will attempt to discuss some of these here, for a more thorough discussion, you are encouraged to consult my earlier book, *Pathways to Intimacy: Conversations for Closeness – Creating the marriage you have always dreamed of.*

Support Network

It is important that you and your spouse reach out to selected individuals for support, guidance, and advice. This is a difficult place for both of you to be and you should not attempt to take the journey alone. Some words of caution at this point are probably necessary and hopefully, beneficial. First, you and your spouse should not seek out another couple to serve as confidants in this matter. It would unnecessarily put them in a difficult position as husband and wife and as your friends.

The sense of divided loyalties would be significant. Second, choose people who will not tell everyone they know about your situation and personal life. Third, select people that you trust; people that you know will impart wisdom and knowledge. Fourth, avoid family members that could harbor negative feelings towards your spouse as a result of the infidelity and whose subsequent thoughts and behaviors could negatively impact the relationship in the future. For example, a wife whose husband had an affair may not want to tell her parents because it would likely damage their relationship with the husband for the remainder of their lives. You should attempt to have 1-3 people that you involve at a closer level and perhaps another 2-3 that you can call if necessary.

Key Issues

Trust

Trust is probably the thing that takes the most patience and is the most challenging and complex part of rebuilding the marriage following an infidelity. As I stated in an earlier chapter, I believe that most couples enter into a relationship wanting and willing to trust one another. Except in those cases where one or both partners have been hurt previously by a boyfriend, girlfriend, or spouse, they should be able to trust one another from the beginning of the relationship. When an affair or infidelity occurs however, the trust factor diminishes rapidly and the injured partner is left no longer trusting his or her spouse. Trust can come back in cases such as this, but it takes dedicated effort, commitment, and patience on the part of both individuals.

The first place to start in rebuilding trust is for the person that was unfaithful to cease all contact with the other person or to get rid of objects associated with the behavior. For example, if the person was engaged in pornography and masturbation, he or she should dispose of all pornography (hard copy and/or electronic files) and have their spouse install any desired passwords, filters, or locks that he or she is comfortable with. In extreme cases, they may even want to get rid of the computer all together. This may sound extreme, but you must prove that you are willing to do whatever it takes – and that the marriage is more important. If the behavior involves strip clubs, adult book stores, massage parlors, or escort services, you must completely stop going to these places and should avoid those general areas of town so as to avoid any perception that you are still acting out. If there is an affair partner in real life, on the internet, or via text and phone, you must end the relationship and be willing to do so in front of your spouse or at least show him or her evidence that you actually did. Evidence may be a text message, e-mail, letter, or proof that a call was made to their number. I realize that this proof is not absolute, but it is a start. It is possible that you could still secretly maintain contact, but the hope is that you won't. If you do, that would likely be the last straw and you might as well count on your spouse leaving and the marriage being over. Cutting off all contact with the affair partner is non-negotiable. If it is someone you work with, you may even have to look for alternate employment.

The critical element in rebuilding trust in the relationship is to not do anything that would give your spouse reason to not trust you or that would further destroy any small amount of trust that has developed in the recovery process. To do this, you must be completely honest with one another. The person that had the affair must be an open book. Everything should be completely transparent and made available for further scrutiny and examination as desired. This is difficult because the injured partner doesn't want to treat their spouse like a child or have to question every behavior. The betraying partner doesn't want to live their life under a microscope with everything they do being scrutinized. You must be honest and sincere in everything you say and do. A simple example might be that if you tell your husband or wife that you will be home by a certain time, then you need to be home by that time. If for some reason you can't, you should call your spouse ahead of time, explain why you are going to be late and tell them what time you will be home. Your reason for being late must be logical and honest. You should also offer to show your spouse anything they feel the need to see. This may include cell phone text and call records, e-mail and internet browser history, and even the inside of your vehicle (including mileage).

Checking behaviors such as these are often referred to as co-dependent behaviors in the addiction world, but you need to recognize that your spouse has been severely hurt. He or she does not trust you yet. As the trust starts to develop, their need to engage in these behaviors will diminish. Eventually, they should stop these behaviors completely and if you continue to be open and honest in everything you do, giving your spouse no reason not to trust you, then you should also see the trust come back to normal levels. I use the word normal to indicate a level that is healthy and functional, but not necessarily at a hundred percent. That will likely take additional time and it may never completely get to that point. You or your spouse has been hurt in such a way that the fear of it happening again and a subsequent sliver of doubt may always exist, thus making complete trust a very optimistic, if not unrealistic goal. This does not mean you don't have a great marriage at this point; it simply means that you are human and that there is still some work to do. There is no such thing as a perfect marriage. There is always room for improvement.

Forgiveness

Forgiveness involves several different elements. First, the person that had the affair must forgive themselves. You are probably wondering why this is important and perhaps how it is even possible. I am of the opinion that a person who is stuck in the guilt and shame associated with their behavior will have a very difficult, if not impossible time moving on. If you are the one that had the affair, I recommend that you attempt to recognize that although you did a really bad thing, you are human and that all humans make mistakes. I am not trying to minimize the behavior, but rather, to highlight the process of repentance, change, and growth. People deserve second chances if they are truly willing to address the causes of the behavior and change. It will require considerable effort however. As the saying goes, "When the going gets tough; the tough get going."

I would also encourage you to seek out your clergy if you are religious. This person can help you find peace and comfort as you discover a deeper relationship with God. This person would be considered a key part of your support network discussed earlier. Building a stronger relationship with God will not only help you forgive yourself, but will help you obtain and understand God's forgiveness better as well. The twelve steps talk about making amends to people that you have harmed through your addiction. Although you may not be dealing with an addiction, it is important to begin considering who you have harmed through your actions and prepare to make amends where possible to do so.

The concept of making amends transitions us to the third element of forgiveness – that of seeking forgiveness from others. When you engaged in the affair, one of the people you hurt is your affair partner and possibly his or her family. Making amends and seeking forgiveness from this person is probably not reasonable since you have cut off all contact. Reestablishing contact, even for such a seemingly good reason, would potentially undermine all the hard work and effort expended thus far. The risk is simply too great.

The primary person you need to seek forgiveness from is your spouse. You have hurt him or her greatly and you need to communicate to them that you understand the pain you have caused, that you are truly sorry for your actions, and that you are going to do everything in your power to prevent it from happening again. I would suggest writing out a letter of apology to your spouse and once you have it exactly as you want it and it says what is weighing heavily upon your heart, set up a time when the two of you can be alone and share it with them. You should not rush this process and it should not happen until you clearly understand how your actions hurt your partner and can communicate a deep understanding of this to your spouse. You should schedule plenty of time to have a discussion about your letter and its content and you should offer to give your letter to your spouse when finished. If done correctly and at the right time, this letter can have a profound impact upon the rebuilding process.

In addition to your spouse, you will want to seek forgiveness from key family members on both sides of the family that have been made aware of the situation. Depending on distance, this may be accomplished via e-mail or letter, but will likely be more meaningful if done in person. The key is to communicate that you made a mistake; that you dishonored yourself, your spouse, and the family; that you are a different person now; that you will do everything possible to live up to the values expected of you as a husband and father; and that you will do all that is necessary to regain their respect.

Healthy Sexuality

This section is titled healthy sexuality because the key point is for the couple to understand the importance of healthy sexuality within the marriage. It begins by having a discussion of the sacredness of each other's body and the rich blessing that comes from opportunities to enjoy and experience the uniqueness of our partner's sexuality. It is not meant for others to share. It is reserved for each other and should be considered a wonderful and extraordinary gift. We are complacent in American society with respect to sexuality and as a result, risk making sex routine and insignificant. It has often become a need to be fulfilled instead of a means of expressing love.

Couples should discuss their sexuality. You may find this difficult following an affair or infidelity and that is precisely why you need to begin having these types of discussions. You may want to start by discussing the fact that you don't want to be sexual and maybe don't even want to be touched. You may not even want to sleep in the same bed, or even the same room. That is okay. I have counseled many individuals and couples who felt this way. The important thing is to begin sharing your feelings about it so that you can start moving forward as a couple.

Start slow and do only what feels comfortable. You may start by sitting on opposite ends of the couch one day only to find yourselves making passionate love days, weeks, or months later. Communicate to each other what feels comfortable and good, as well as what doesn't. On the opposite end of the continuum, you must resist the urge to become hypersexual in an effort to "keep" or satisfy a spouse who has been cheating. It will not work and it is degrading for you.

Rebuilding your sexual relationship will be a work in progress and must be taken at a pace that is acceptable to both you and your spouse. The problem is not the sex, but rather, the intimacy. That being said, you will need to develop a new closeness. You will have to rediscover one another in a safe and secure environment. You may have to start by simply holding hands. I once had a couple that could only tolerate touching fingers; even holding hands was too overwhelming. They began by literally putting their index fingers together. Your initial efforts will ultimately develop into more sexual forms of touching and foreplay until you are finally ready for intercourse.

One technique designed to take some of the pressure off of being sexual often recommended in sex therapy involves sitting or lying next to one another, slowly touching and exploring each other's body in a non-sexual way.

To do this, you will want to agree that intercourse is not an option, as well as touching specific sexual areas of the body. This exercise will progress over time until you are paying attention to these areas and ultimately, should involve intercourse. If done right, sexual responsiveness to one another will increase, but so will intimacy and safety. For more information on this and related techniques, I would recommend that you go to your local bookstore or search online for books on healthy sexuality. The important point is that healthy sexuality is about safety and intimacy.

Another discussion couples need to have pertaining to sex pertains to what behaviors are considered acceptable sexually and who makes that decision. Personally, I feel that couples should strive to keep their relationship exciting, passionate, and spontaneous; but they should agree on what things they do together and neither of them should be exposed to something that could harm, injure, or humiliate them. As mentioned earlier, other people should not be part of the sexual relationship as the focus needs to be on exclusivity. Fantasy and role-play can be a great thing, but not if it involves other people. Statements and beliefs such as this may run counter to modern societal messages regarding sexual behavior and may even sound prudish, but the last thing a couple recovering from infidelity needs is more sexual partners. Regardless of personal beliefs about what is right or wrong, the relationship is simply too fragile.

The couple should strive to develop a sexual relationship that demonstrates love and respect for one another. Truly seek to understand and learn more about your spouse's body and what pleases him or her. The goal should be mutual enjoyment that is grounded in pleasure. Each of you should strive to provide a meaningful and pleasurable sexual experience for your spouse. As stated earlier, start slow and progress according to your mutual desires and associated comfort level. Be patient with yourselves and with one another. Give yourself permission to go slow and seek ways to build intimacy and connectedness.

Intimacy

Intimacy is a topic that is typically misunderstood. Many people make a direct correlation between intimacy and sexuality. Intimacy does not have to involve sex, and many people have sexual relationships with little intimacy. Intimacy is more about emotional connectedness and closeness than it is about anything physical or sexual. That is why emotional infidelity is so devastating – it involves a significant level of intimacy. Women are especially sensitive to this type of behavior because it crosses the line into something that is truly reserved for the married couple – even beyond that of a sexual relationship. The two go together however because most women will not enter into a sexual relationship with someone unless an acceptable level of intimacy is present. Men, on the other hand, are wired differently and can enter into a sexual relationship that is in their mind, purely and completely sexual. They can compartmentalize their life and relationships into nice little pieces where each part is separate and distinct from all the others. For men, intimacy is optional, and sometimes even discouraged.

Intimacy develops when two people share their lives with one another. This can be on a verbal level such as when you and your spouse sit down and really talk to each other, sharing your hopes, dreams, ambitions, and desires with one another. This is why regular communication with each another as a couple is so important. You can also share your lives by doing things together. Find things that you both enjoy and do them together. This does not mean you can't have individual hobbies, but look for things to do together as well. If you like to play golf, perhaps your wife or husband would enjoy learning to play with you. Many couples enjoy watching television or movies together. Cuddling up with each other on the couch while watching a good movie is a great way to build intimacy in your relationship. If you both like different types of movies, resist the temptation to do your own thing and instead, take turns picking the movie. Spend time outside together. A great way to build intimacy is to exercise together. This may involve such activities as running, swimming, bicycling, hiking, rock climbing, and camping. While not all activities will seem appealing, there is bound to be some that do.

It is important that you spend time going out together as a couple. Almost every couple I have counseled following an affair or infidelity stated that a major contributor was not spending enough time together. I recommend that all couples go on a date weekly. This means as a couple – without the kids. There will be time for family activities as well, but these dates are only for you as a couple. If money or babysitting is an obstacle, simply go places that don't cost as much. For example, a picnic in the park and a walk on the beach can make a great date. It shows your romantic side, while also being inexpensive. It also gives you plenty of time to talk and grow closer in your relationship.

To combat the babysitter issue, I would recommend getting to know other couples and after you get to know some of them fairly well, raise the idea of trading babysitting so that both couples have opportunities to go out. This is a great way to find quality babysitting without it costing you a cent. In addition to weekly date nights, it is also important for couples to get away overnight as a couple. Although sex may be a natural and wonderful byproduct of the experience, the real benefit is the impact on intimacy. I had a friend once tell me that the best thing he and his wife had started doing for their marriage was getting a hotel room once every couple of months. Although this sometimes included travel, they would oftentimes just get a room in town at a local hotel. They would bring the kids over during the day and let them go swimming, and then they would spend the evenings and nights alone. He was surprised at how much the kids enjoyed it and was amazed by how much it truly improved his marital relationship.

Another way to develop intimacy is to learn how to touch each other and do things that the other enjoys. This can include a massage, preparing a bath for your wife, rubbing each other's feet, taking a bath or shower together, sitting together in a hot tub without clothes (if you have one), or just lying in bed naked holding each other. These things can be fun and will dramatically enhance the level of intimacy in your relationship. Start where you feel comfortable and work up from there. The key is to focus on the needs and desires of your spouse.

My wife is a great example of a woman who uses touch to increase intimacy in our relationship. She loves to be held and since I am aware of that fact, I try to give her plenty of hugs and to hold her whenever possible. In return she will oftentimes give me a massage or rub my feet – much to the objection of my daughters who find this somewhat disgusting and think I am spoiled. She also loves to cuddle and just be held – whether it is on the couch or in bed. Again, I am happy to oblige. I also like to rub her shoulders and run my hands over her body. She appreciates this and it increases intimacy.

One final point regarding intimacy pertains to technology. Many of the devices we have in our lives today are a barrier and an obstacle to intimacy. Having your cell phone ringing while you are trying to spend time together is not going to increase intimacy. Do not try to make and receive calls while also trying to spend time with your spouse. The same can be said with texting, e-mail, and a host of other activities. Consider turning these devices off or putting them away during the time you are trying to spend together as a couple. I heard an announcer on a popular Christian radio station once say that her family goes as far as to have a technologically free day once a week. This is a day where they turn off all technology (including radio and television) and spend time doing things together as a family. She stated that it has been great and that the kids, although resistant at first, really seem to enjoy it. Eliminate distractions and barriers to intimacy. This is why retreats, camping, and isolated resorts can be great for relationships – they strip away the complexities of life and simplify things.

The Negative Cycle

Although there are many reasons why an individual will have an affair and cheat on their spouse, I believe that these reasons can be grouped into a category I will simply refer to as emotional neglect. A behavioral pattern develops that subsequently results in a negative cycle of interaction that intensifies feelings of neglect and abandonment, as well as potential lack of appreciation and feelings that one is unloved. In other words, they fail to have their emotional needs met in the marital relationship.

Let's look at a hypothetical example. Dave and Jennifer are both in their early thirties. They have been married for seven years and have two young children, ages five and three. Dave is the regional manager of a large retail chain. Jennifer is a stay-at-home mother and housewife. Prior to having children however, she had what she describes as "a very enjoyable career and a nice income" as an office manager in a prestigious law firm. Dave's hours at work have been getting longer and longer. He is struggling to even make it home before the kids go to bed. Jennifer has stated on many occasions that she feels like a single mom, having to do everything on her own.

When Dave does finally make it home, he is worn out. He and Jennifer barely talk or interact in any real or meaningful way. They have not made love in weeks and Jennifer feels that work has become more important to Dave than she is. He does not notice the work she does around the house and the only comments he makes are negative ones. She told a male friend recently that she feels very lonely and unappreciated; something she has had difficulty telling her husband due to the lack of time they spend together and his emotional unresponsiveness to her.

Dave, on the other hand, feels that he is working very hard to build a better future for his family. He even describes the long hours as "an investment on the future." He goes on to say that his efforts and resultant sacrifice go virtually unnoticed by his wife. He describes his welcome home each evening as "an assault", in which Jennifer goes into a tirade about how she has to do everything and begins "nagging" him about doing more. He describes feeling "disrespected and unappreciated" for what he does. When this happens, he usually withdraws into the den or living room where he turns on the television and allows himself to be absorbed by whatever show or movie that happens to be on. It has become a nightly escape from his wife. When he engages in this isolating form of behavior however, Jennifer begins to feel increasingly lonely and unloved.

One night, instead of turning on the television, he decided to turn on the computer and watch some porn. After viewing a couple of short videos, he decided that to masturbate as well. A couple of nights later, remembering that the porn and masturbation were much better than television, he returned to the computer. Recalling some guys in the office talking about a hot adult dating site, he decided to check that out. He developed a profile and began chatting with a couple of women on the site who happened to live nearby. The chatting continued for a few days and then he started texting and talking to one of these women on the phone.

One night, after a rather stressful day and a bad argument with Jennifer, Dave decided to meet this woman for drinks. She was beautiful and seemed completely interested in him and his work. She was exciting to talk to and be around and made him feel really good about himself. The evening ended with them getting a hotel room and having sex. They continued to see each other on a regular basis for the next three or four months, having sex at least a couple of times per week. The time Dave was physically spending with this other woman, as well as talking, e-mailing, texting, and fantasizing about her had a significant impact on his career. The quality and quantity of his work had diminished so much in fact, that he was severely reprimanded and even threatened with termination. Jennifer eventually discovered the affair and confronted Dave about it. They are now in counseling.

The negative cycle that this couple has created is making it virtually impossible for them to meet each other's emotional needs. As demonstrated in the case example, the resultant emotional neglect made it relatively easy for an affair or other form of infidelity to occur. It could have happened with Dave or Jennifer – he just happened to create the opportunity first. It would have been really easy for Jennifer to cheat on Dave with the male friend she began confiding in or some other man that happened to take an interest in her.

It might be helpful at this point to summarize the negative cycle that Dave and Jennifer have developed. By coming home late, not helping around the house, and spending little to no quality time with his wife, Jennifer had begun to feel unloved, unappreciated, and neglected. She then responded by attacking and nagging Dave, making him feel unappreciated, inadequate, and disrespected. Dave withdrew from Jennifer, isolating himself through television and the computer. This intensified Jennifer's feelings of neglect, lack of appreciation, and feeling unloved. She eventually began to give up, continuing to expend energy in the kids and the home, while also beginning to confide in a male friend. If this continues it is likely that an affair with this person could easily develop (at least an emotional one). In this case however, Dave crossed the line of infidelity first through his actions on the computer (pornography, masturbation, e-mail, and chatting) which escalated into an offline sexual relationship.

It is much easier to sit back and see the dynamics associated with the negative cycle when it is on paper than it is when you are in the midst of actually living it. The important question now becomes, "what do we do to fix it?" Knowing what is wrong is only half the battle; the difficult part is taking that information and making things better. In the case of Dave and Jennifer, there are some relatively simple steps that can be taken to make things good again. First, knowing that Jennifer feels neglected, unloved, and unappreciated, Dave could start by trying to come home earlier and spend additional time with her. They could start going out together one night a week. He could also come home and cook dinner for them, run a bath for her, and while she is enjoying the bath, spend time doing the dishes and taking care of the kids. He should also compliment her on the house, her cooking, and how she cares for the children; showing a sincere appreciation for her efforts during the day. He should also acknowledge her sacrifice and how important it is for them as a family to have her at home. He should try to increase the intimacy and passion between them as a couple by perhaps holding and touching her more. He needs to find out what she wants either indirectly through observation or directly by asking her. Finally, he must refrain from isolating when he comes home, thus shutting Jennifer out by turning on the television or computer.

Jennifer could help Dave by showing more appreciation for the work he does outside the home. I have had many husbands tell me that they wished their wife would thank them once in a while for what they do at work, earning a living, and providing for the family. Many wives don't do this, contending that at least their husband gets to go to work and interact with adults. Jennifer could also find a better way of encouraging Dave to help out more around the house. Her assertive, even aggressive and hostile method of attacking and belittling him is simply counterproductive and results in Dave feeling disrespected by his wife (someone that he should feel nurtured and loved by) in his own home (a place that should feel safe and secure).

Jennifer might also want to consider offering Dave some time to be alone, to wind down following work. Many men thrive on this as they need to retreat for a short time to their "cave." By offering him that time, Jennifer will be reaching out to him in an attempt to meet his need for solitude. He will feel validated and will appreciate her more for the gesture. He will then likely be more attentive towards her, responding to her in a healthier, more loving, and affectionate manner.

As you can see from this example, it is extremely easy for a couple to enter into a negative cycle which subsequently results in the two individuals experiencing unmet needs and a host of negative feelings. As the couple interacts, the negative behavioral patterns will cause the overall relationship to spiral downward, out of control. This will continue until such time that it turns into a physical altercation, or they begin to turn from one another through a pattern of withdrawal and isolation. Ultimately, if this persists, they will continue to withdraw into the arms of another person or engage in other inappropriate behavior. By replacing the negative behaviors with positive ones, the couple can reinforce feelings of love, respect, appreciation, and concern; thus enabling both partners to have their emotional needs met through a happy and loving marriage. This positive cycle becomes a means of increasing intimacy and is the best way for preventing and even recovering from infidelity in the marriage.

Exercise

Questions for Consideration: Answer each question to the best of your ability, being as thorough as possible in your response.

1. Describe your negative cycle in as much detail as possible. Describe the specific behaviors, thoughts, and feelings involved.

2. Taking the negative cycle into consideration, what would a positive cycle look like? Be specific. Discuss thing that would particularly improve intimacy within the marriage.

3. Discuss the factors that you feel contributed to the affair or infidelity. In other words, why did it occur? What can you do to ensure that these factors will no longer be a problem?

4. Taking into consideration those things that were discussed in this chapter, what have you found most helpful and why? How might having an understanding of the rebuilding phase of recovery from infidelity help you in your relationship today?

CHAPTER TEN

Phase Six – Maintenance

Transitioning to the Maintenance Phase

After some period of time, a couple recovering from infidelity will transition from a rebuilding phase to a maintenance phase. How long the rebuilding phase will last is dependent on many factors and varies from couple to couple. On average however, I would not anticipate seeing a couple enter the maintenance phase earlier than 6-12 months. The key factors that will let you know that you are ready to enter the maintenance phase include the following:

- The affair or infidelity is not brought up during regular conversation, disagreements, or arguments

- There has been no contact with the affair partner since discovery and subsequent confrontation of the affair or infidelity

- The individual that had the affair has been able to find self-forgiveness

- The injured partner has forgiven his or her spouse for the affair

- The couple has sought out and utilized a reasonable support network as appropriate

- The couple has achieved therapeutic goals in individual, couple, and group counseling as applicable

- The injured partner no longer feels the need to engage in checking behaviors (e.g., cell phone, e-mail, calling the spouse's place of employment etc.)

- Both partners would say that trust has been restored to acceptable levels

- Both partners would describe the relationship as fulfilling physically and emotionally

- The couple has discovered the root issues leading to the affair (intrapersonal and relational) and have taken the necessary steps to fix these issues

The maintenance phase is a period of stabilization. It involves monitoring and engaging one another as necessary to keep the relationship in a healthy place and to prevent future infidelity. This phase of recovery from infidelity consists of many specific behaviors already mentioned or discussed in previous phases of infidelity recovery. The difference with this particular phase however, is that the tools are applied strategically as necessary in response to changing situations and dynamics. For example, assume that you recognize that you are arguing more often or that you have become more distant over time. A proactive response would be to discuss this with your spouse, brainstorming potential reasons for the shift. You should then contact your therapist and arrange to see him or her for some marital counseling (possibly 2-3 sessions). These sessions would serve as a "booster shot" or preventive measure. I have heard some describe it as being similar to hearing a small noise in your car and deciding to take it to a mechanic just to have it looked at. You want to be sure that things are alright, and if not, you want to contain or minimize the damage.

The key element in the maintenance phase is to be attentive to yourself, each other, and the marriage by continuously assessing the overall health of each individual in the relationship, as well as the marital relationship itself. When something seems wrong or could possibly head in that direction, action is warranted. As another example, assume that you are the one that had an affair. It has been two years and the relationship seems to be going really well now. Without warning, you receive a message from an old girlfriend or boyfriend on a social networking site asking if you would like to meet up for dinner and drinks. You would love to see this person again as you dated for all four years of high school. You are also keenly aware that since this individual messaged you on a site your spouse has access to; there is a very strong likelihood that he or she will see the message as well. You are almost positive that this message will upset your spouse and trigger bad memories and feelings pertaining to the infidelity. Armed with this information, you must not wait for your world to crumble around you.

A reasonable response would be to immediately call your spouse and let them know what just happened. Send a response to this person telling them that you are unable to meet and that considering the nature of your past relationship and the fact that you are now happily married, it just would not be a good idea. Show this message to your spouse. Depending on his or her reaction at this point, you may want to suggest that you each go to a couple sessions of individual and/or marital counseling to work through any issues that this situation triggered. You may also want to spend extra time together as a couple, intentionally being more attentive to each other's emotional needs and desires. Engaging in activities specifically designed to increase relational intimacy would be extremely helpful. There are many things that you could do. The key is to do something; doing nothing is not an option. You have a large tool bag filled with a variety of tools. Many options exist; select at least one.

I believe it is wise in the first 3-5 years following an infidelity for the couple to stay engaged in counseling activities. This may consist of one or two sessions every couple of months or possibly a weekend retreat or couple intensive. I personally feel that retreats are great during this phase because it gives the couple an opportunity to spend time alone, while also providing structure and material for working on the relationship. It also sends the message to each other that "our marriage is important to me." Attending a one-day or weekend workshop may be another possibility. I would recommend programs such as *Laugh you way to a Better Marriage*. The material is outstanding and the cost is extremely reasonable.

Similarly, I believe that each individual should participate in counseling for themselves and may even want to consider attending an individual retreat or similar activity. Local churches and religious non-profit organizations such as Promise Keepers are a good resource. They typically organize and facilitate structured programs that are gender specific.

Physical, Emotional, and Spiritual Health

Stability and maintenance following an infidelity involves paying close attention to your physical, emotional, and spiritual health. The more developed these areas of your life are, the more successful your recovery will be. For example, when it comes to your physical self, you must get adequate rest; eat healthy, nutritional meals; and get plenty of exercise. You must also go to the doctor regularly for periodic physicals and to address any health issues that you might begin to notice. Tied to your physical health is also the need for a healthy sex life.

Your emotional health has more to do with relationships. These include your marriage, as well as friendships and family relationships. Additionally, it takes into account your relationship with your children as applicable, and with those you work for and with. These relationships are important and it is strongly recommended that we have friendships with others apart from our spouse, as well as together as a couple. We should attend to our friendships and try to nurture them where and when possible. Emotional health may also include maintaining our need for attention, affection, and intimacy within the marriage. We need to engage in hobbies and other activities that bring us enjoyment and keep us grounded. My wife loves to read and crochet. I read, but that is not necessarily a source of great enjoyment. I would actually rather write a book than read one. I definitely don't crochet and it is a safe bet to say that I probably never will. I love to watch football;

action movies; and television shows such as *Law and Order*, *Two and a Half Men*, and *Army Wives*. In fact, my wife and I have made watching *Army Wives* a weekly ritual and it is something we truly look forward to doing together. I enjoy going to the gym, jogging, swimming, and bicycling. I also enjoy riding my motorcycle, but have recognized the need to find friends to do this with. Riding alone just isn't that much fun.

Oftentimes, we ignore or neglect our spiritual self. We have become a society that has little respect or use for God in our lives. This is a very sad and even disappointing thing as God is an incredible source of strength and love. Our lives, individually and collectively, are made better through a committed relationship with God and through active worship. I have heard many people say that "a couple that prays together stays together." I urge you not to dismiss this thought prematurely. Couples that have a strong relationship with God are better prepared to weather the challenges of life and do appear to have better marriages.

I enjoy going to church and Sunday school with my wife. In the past, we have participated in a nightly devotional – as a family and as a couple. The resultant discussions have been wonderful. I also enjoy the times that we have knelt down together in prayer – thanking God and asking Him to continue to bless our lives. There is a powerful spirit that will fill your heart when you humbly kneel down with your spouse, holding his or her hands in yours and asking God to join you in this incredible relationship. Try it – you will be amazed by the results. I also think husbands and wives should participate in ministries that enable them to be around other men and women as applicable. I find a great strength in being around other men that love God and that despite their personal imperfections and defects, are trying to embrace God, and live a value-centered life as a father, husband, and as a man of God.

You may be saying to yourself, "This all sounds great, but doing these things is not easy. There just isn't enough time in the day, week, month, or year for all these things." I concur on that point – if we don't prioritize and manage our time well. Priorities will shift – and should – as we try to keep our physical, emotional, and spiritual lives in order. We should seek to achieve and maintain balance between these critical life areas, adjusting as necessary to make sure that proper attention is devoted to each as appropriate. For example, if I am doing a lot of things to take care of myself physically, but am ignoring my relationships, or my church life, then I need to adjust in such a way that I can spend more time with friends and family, particularly in the context of worship and spiritual growth.

Let's examine things that can be done in each of these areas as your progress through the maintenance phase of your recovery from infidelity. For each area, these are things you may want to consider as ways to maintain balance in your life and achieve your goals. The list is not all-inclusive.

Physical

- Go to bed at a reasonable time and get up at a reasonable time. There is good advice in the concept "early to bed, early to rise."

- Eat three balanced meals a day and avoid unnecessary or excessive snacking

- Limit use of alcohol

- Avoid tobacco and other harmful substances

- Make regular doctor visits as appropriate

- Ensure you get adequate exercise. A reasonable goal would be 1-2 hours of cardio 3-4 times per week

- Practice good hygiene

- Do not take unnecessary physical risks

- Make a dedicated effort to maintain a healthy, happy, and active sex life

- Spend time outside working in the yard and doing things you enjoy

- Have hobbies – individually and together as a couple

Emotional

- Spend time every day with your spouse doing things that you enjoy

- Spend time every day having meaningful discussions with your spouse

- Spend quality time whenever possible as a family and with your children

- Make sure you have friends that you spend time with on a regular basis (individually and as a couple)

- Participate in hobbies and other fulfilling activities

- Nurture your relationships with your parents, siblings, and other extended family members

- Make reasonable efforts to see relatives on a regular basis when possible

- Utilize social media and other technology to stay in touch with people as it is prudent to do so

- Nurture wok relationships so that work can be more fulfilling and meaningful to you

- Go on a date night once per week

- Go away with your spouse as a couple overnight at least once every two months

- Do things that will keep your mind active (e.g., reading, puzzles, games, enrolling in a college course, or learning a new skill or activity)

- Nurture your sexual relationship and intentionally make physical intimacy and affection a regular part of your day

Spiritual

- Join a local church, synagogue, temple etc. Finding the right one that best fits the needs of your family may take some time – be patient

- Participate in regular worship (weekly worship celebration services, Sunday school, Bible study etc.)

- Join a life group as a couple. Most larger churches offer these throughout the week and include various themes or topics

- Become a prayer warrior – make it a regular part of your life

- Join with your spouse in daily prayer as a couple and ads a family

- Join with your spouse in a daily devotional as a couple

- Participate in regular ministry activities for men or women as applicable

- Look for ways to serve your community as a family

- Consider domestic or international mission trips as a family or couple

- Spend adequate time in nature – being influenced by and a part of God's creation

- Participate in regular individual, couple, and family scripture study

As you become more grounded in your recovery from infidelity and perhaps more experienced as different types of situations arise, you will develop a greater appreciation and understanding of the types of tools that can and must be implemented to keep you and your relationship healthy. Most of these measures are preventive in nature, meaning that if you are applying these tools on a regular basis, you should stay relatively centered and on track. The larger deviations will come as you stop doing these things. Again, it is important to assess your daily life and evaluate the physical – emotional – spiritual balance. If sex addiction is a factor in the infidelity, then the maintenance phase will be more extensive and structured. See chapter four in this book for more information pertaining to sexual addiction.

Exercise

Questions for Consideration: Answer each question to the best of your ability, being as thorough as possible in your response.

1. Describe how you will take care of yourself _physically_ during the maintenance phase of your recovery from infidelity.

2. Describe how you will take care of yourself _emotionally_ during the maintenance phase of your recovery from infidelity.

3. Describe how you will take care of yourself _spiritually_ during the maintenance phase of your recovery from infidelity.

4. Taking into consideration those things that were discussed in this chapter, what have you found most helpful and why? How might having an understanding of the maintenance phase of recovery from infidelity help you in your relationship today?

Part III

FINDING HOPE

CHAPTER ELEVEN

Author Reflections

Personal Reflections from the Author

As we bring this book to a close, I feel that I still need and want to say a few more things to you. Although it is likely that I do not know you, it is possible that I do. Perhaps you are a family member, a friend, or a client. Maybe we attend the same church, our children go to the same school, or we have kids on the same little league team. I hope that is the case. I would love to talk to you more about your situation and get your thoughts about the helpfulness of this book. Regardless of whether we have ever met or not, I do know many people like you – people who have been devastated by the effects of infidelity and/or sexual addiction and are trying earnestly to rebuild their lives and their relationships. Recovery is a very long and difficult road. You will face challenges and obstacles along the way that will discourage, dishearten, and depress you. You will lose sight of hope and will want to just give up. Be persistent and stay the course. Endure until the very end.

My assumption is that you are reading this book because you and your spouse are recovering from an affair or infidelity, or have experienced one and are contemplating recovery. It is also possible that you aren't sure if your husband or wife has cheated on you, but you perhaps think so. Regardless, I am thankful you are reading this book and I hope that it has been helpful to you. I have tried to give you important information; while speaking to you in a practical, down-to-earth manner; offering you tools that have hopefully been useful to you in your recovery from infidelity.

You are going through one of the most difficult situations an individual and couple can go through. You have been flooded and overwhelmed with emotions, and have had to deal with incredibly difficult questions such as: should I leave or should I stay? Who should I tell? Should I leave my wife (or husband) for this other person? What will people think? Am I imagining all of this?

I have tried to give you the information and tools necessary to find answers to many of these questions, as well as steps to take to recover from infidelity should you choose to do so. It is my sincere desire that you will. You cannot change the past; the affair or infidelity you have experienced is unfortunate, but it is real and it has happened. What you can change however, is the future. Hopefully this book has helped you want to do that, while also helping you figure out how you might accomplish this. You and your spouse have the destiny of your future in your hands. You will ultimately determine what path you will take and the impact it will have on your family's future.

I have witnessed many couples recover from infidelity – personally and professionally. I have had couples towards the end of counseling tell me that they felt as though the affair was perhaps the best thing that ever happened in their marriage because it helped them to identify things they needed to work on and subsequently made their relationship better and stronger as a result. I used to buy into this statement, but I know better now. Yes, their relationship is better because they have worked through many different problem areas in their marriage. That is a great and wonderful thing. Nobody will argue this point. What I disagree with however, is the idea that the affair itself was somehow a good thing.

Infidelity, of any kind, is never a good thing. Let me say that again. Infidelity, of any kind, is never a good thing. The truly positive outcome is that these couples decided to take a risk and embark on a journey of recovery and by doing so, their marriage is better – perhaps even better than it has ever been. It is unfortunate that it sometimes takes something as devastating and traumatic as an infidelity to get individuals and couples to understand the seriousness of the situation. I would like to think that we all truly desire a great marriage and that we would be willing to do anything humanly possible to achieve that goal. As you contemplate the road ahead, I sincerely hope that you will consider taking the necessary risk and decide to embark on a journey that has the potential to heal your relationship in miraculous and astonishing ways. You will never know what is possible unless you attempt the seemingly impossible. I want the very best for you and your family. You are in my thoughts and in my prayers.

Author Biography

Dr. Michael Howard is a Licensed Professional Counselor, Clinical Addictions Specialist, Marriage and Family Therapist and Mental Health Counselor. He is experienced in individual, couple, family, and group therapy. His counseling specialties include couples therapy, infidelity, sexual addiction, and trauma recovery. Dr Howard is currently the Executive Director and founder of Healing Solutions Counseling Center, PLLC in Charlotte, NC.

Dr. Howard holds masters degrees in professional counseling, addiction psychology, marriage and family therapy, and discipleship ministries. He also holds a Doctor of Education (EdD) degree in counseling psychology. He is a Board Certified Professional Christian Counselor and a Certified Sex Addiction Therapist and Supervisor. He is also a Clinical Member and Approved Supervisor with the American Association for Marriage and Family Therapy (AAMFT).

Dr. Howard is an adjunct faculty member in the marriage and family therapy graduate program at Northcentral University in Prescott Valley, Arizona where he teaches courses in marriage and family therapy, sexual addiction and infidelity, treatment of military families, and sex therapy. He has also taught undergraduate courses in psychology at Campbell University at Marine Corps Base Camp Lejeune, located near Jacksonville, NC.

Dr. Howard has served in the United States Navy as both a nuclear-trained submarine electrician (Chief Petty Officer) for 18 years and as a Chaplain for 10 years. He is scheduled to retire in June, 2012. While on active duty, he has served in a Marine combat battalion, at Navy Boot camp, on five different submarines and most recently as Command Chaplain of a Naval warship.

In addition to being a prominent relationship and addiction therapist, Dr. Howard has authored numerous articles for scholarly journals and has presented at National conferences and to general audiences throughout the country on the topics of ethics, sexual addiction, infidelity, and building fulfilling relationships. He is the author of the book, *Pathways to Intimacy: Conversations for Closeness – Creating the Marriage you have always Dreamed of.*

Dr. Howard has been married for more than 25 years to the love of his life, Lonna. They have four children (Ila, Dawn, Kimberly, and Jonathan), and two dogs. He enjoys jogging, working out at the gym, camping, biking, and spending time with his family.

Made in the USA
Lexington, KY
27 April 2017